LOGGING FOR THE COMPANY

LOGGING FOR THE COMPANY

Marcus Daly and Flume Logging Near Anaconda, 1883–1917

Jack Losensky

sweetgrassbooks
a division of Farcountry Press

Library of Congress Control Number: 2023917428

ISBN 978-1-59152-337-6

Design by Sue Murray

Front cover, top left: Photograph courtesy of the University of Montana Archives and Special Collections (77-140); **top right:** photograph courtesy of Mile High Nordic Ski Education Foundation; **bottom left:** photograph courtesy of University of Montana Archives and Special Collections (77-203); **bottom right:** photograph courtesy of National Archives RG-95-53926

Back cover, left: Photograph Courtesy of Vanna Boccadori at Mount Haggin Wildlife Management Area; **right:** photograph courtesy of the Montana Historical Society Photograph Archives PAC 78-50.5

For more information or to order extra copies of this book call Farcountry Press toll free at (800) 821-3874 or visit www.farcountrypress.com

sweetgrassbooks
a division of Farcountry Press

Produced by Sweetgrass Books
PO Box 5630, Helena, MT 59604; (800) 821-3874; www.sweetgrassbooks.com.

Produced and printed in the United States of America

28 27 26 25 24 2 3 4 5 6

In memory of Donald M. Wood,
who first introduced me to the history of Mt. Haggin

Acknowledgment

I want to express my thanks to Mary Williams and Vanna Boccadori for their willingness to read drafts of my book. Their comments greatly helped to clarify the story I wished to tell. Vanna opened her files and provided historical information on the formation of the Mt. Haggin Wildlife Management Area, as well as a number of photographs which greatly helped visualize the events that transpired here.

Table of Contents

CHAPTER ONE

Development of Mining in the Butte Area

The search for gold was a major driving force to explore vast areas of the West. Once found, thousands of miners, merchants, freighters, and hangers-on descended on the new diggings. They needed wood for shelter, to construct mining facilities, to power their machinery, and to heat their food and their bodies. In the West, much of this demand was supplied by the vast tracts of timber found on the public domain.[1] In areas where major mines were developed, the local supply of wood was soon exhausted and required reaching out to more distant sources. This is the story of how this challenge was met in the silver and copper mines of Butte and Anaconda, Montana.

Prospecting in Montana came about rather late in the development of placer mining in the western United States. The discovery of gold in Idaho Territory in the late 1850s and early 1860s finally brought prospectors into this isolated corner of the world. The pattern that started in the California gold fields played out in Montana as well. After all available areas were staked in the new mining camps, late arrivals were left with a limited number of options. They could buy a claim from one of the established miners, work for wages for a claim holder, go home, or move on to search in a new area. Since these prospectors commonly had spent all their savings to get to the camp, many didn't have the wherewithal to buy a claim. Also, working for a few dollars a day when all that gold was there for the taking if you could find it provided little incentive. Some of the more timid souls, finally realizing the risk to their lives by entering Indian Territory, gave up and returned home. Some were thankful they had survived, while others relived in their minds the adventure they had as they settled into a more peaceful, civilized setting. Still others returned to the failure that had driven them to seek gold in the first place. For many who were unsuccessful, the lure of easy riches was too strong, and this is what drove them over the top of the Rocky Mountains and into unknown Indian Territory, leading to the discovery of the Grasshopper and Alder Gulch diggings in present-day southwest Montana. It was from these camps that parties set out to explore other portions of Montana, leading to the eventual discovery in 1864 of the Silver Bow placers.[2] The placers themselves were not particularly successful and, by 1869, had been pretty well worked out. But what the placers did do was to attract prospectors to the area, and those who had gained experience in the Colorado and Nevada mining areas quickly recognized the high mineralization of the Butte hill. With this recognition came the second phase of development in the Butte area as hard rock mines were developed.

One of the first quartz claims to be worked in the Butte area was the Parrot Lode. Joseph Ramsdell, Billy Parks, Dennis Leary, and Charles Porter built a blast furnace and attempted to extract the silver and other precious metals found on the claim.[3] They had limited success, but did manage to extract a number of wagonloads of matte, which is the sulfide phase of the mineral in the smelting process. They sent this material elsewhere for final refining. At this point the hard realities of their situation settled in. First, their crude extraction process was only marginally successful in extracting the metals from the complicated ores they found. Since the nearest shipping point lay about 400 miles to the south by wagon at Corinne, Utah, the value of the metal they were able to extract was pretty much taken by transportation costs.[4] They also recognized that it would require significant capital which they did not have to develop both the mine and the type of mill that could extract the ores. Subsequently they gave up. A few others tried with similar results and, by the early 1870s, Butte area settlements were pretty much ghost towns. It was not until a new extraction process was developed in the silver mines in Nevada and brought to Butte that efforts were successful in recovering the minerals from the Butte mines. In 1874, William L. Farlin reopened his Travona mine and successfully extracted silver from its ore.[5] A number of other promising mines were also being developed during this same period. These all required significant investment of capital to complete the necessary milling and concentrator facilities to extract the silver and other metals. At about this time, two individuals who had the financial resources to invest in these mines became interested in the opportunities the Butte mines presented. They were Andrew Jackson Davis and William Andrews Clark.

Andrew Jackson Davis was born April 25, 1819, in Massachusetts and at an early age became an errand boy in a store in Boston. He became engaged in the mercantile business and, being a good trader, was quite successful. He eventually settled in Iowaville, Iowa, and built a mill complex and distillery there, which were also successful. After a trip to the gold fields in California, Andrew made a visit to Montana. Recognizing the value of whiskey there, he sent a whole wagon train from his distillery to the territory in 1866, which made him a small fortune. He moved to Gallatin County and was living there in 1870, listed in the census as a speculator that year.[6] He was one of the first men with capital who recognized the potential of the mines at Butte and helped finance one of the efforts in 1868 to mill the complex ores. This effort was unsuccessful. As many of the original claimants lost interest in Butte, he was able to buy up several good claims very cheaply and finally moved to Butte in 1875.[7] Using the new extraction process, he finally was able to recover the minerals from his mines. He eventually bought the Lexington Mine, which proved to be a particularly good silver mine. In the 1880 census he was listed as single and his occupation was in milling and mining.[8] He later sold the Lexington and became a banker in Butte. He died on March 11, 1890, and was the first millionaire in Montana.[9]

Another of the early capitalists was William Andrews Clark, who had established himself in banking in Deer Lodge, Montana. Clark was born on January 8, 1839, in Pennsylvania, but moved with his parents to Iowa in 1856. He attended college and became a teacher in Missouri. With the start of the Civil War and the development of mining activity in Colorado, Clark left Missouri to try his luck at mining. His Colorado adventure was unsuccessful, and he eventually drifted to Bannack, Montana, in 1863, where he developed a placer mine. This mine produced the stake he needed to get into the freighting business to bring supplies from Utah and other points to the mines in Montana. This operation proved successful, and he opened stores in Helena and, later, Deer Lodge, Montana. He also began buying and selling gold and eventually opened a bank in Deer Lodge in 1872. Having developed a strong financial base and also a business that permitted him more free time, he became interested in the mines of Butte. He bought four claims there in 1872 and immediately returned to school to learn more about processing ores, returning to Butte afterward to develop his mines. By 1875, with the backing of Davis and Clark, a number of small stamp mills and a concentrator were constructed and silver, gold, and copper ores were processed successfully from a number of mines in the area.[10]

Into this developing mining area stepped Marcus Daly. Daly was born in Ireland in 1841 and came to America in 1856. He eventually reached Nevada, where he gained experience in silver mining in the Comstock Lode.[11] During his time in Nevada he met and became good friends with fellow miner George Hearst.[12] Daly eventually moved to Utah and became involved with the Walker Brothers, who were bankers, merchants, promoters, and mine owners. In 1872, Daly investigated the Ontario Mine in Utah for the Walker Brothers, but they decided not to buy it. Daly then suggested to Hearst that he should buy the Ontario mine that later became a major contributor to Hearst's fortune.[13] Eventually the Walker Brothers saw some of the ore that was coming from the Butte area and recognized the potential of the mines and decided to invest in the area. In 1876, they sent Daly to investigate the area with instructions that if he found a good looking mine to buy it. A miner by the name of Rolla Butcher had located the Alice Mine in the Butte area around 1875. After inspecting this mine and others, Daly decided the Alice had a great potential and purchased it for the Walker Brothers. Daly was permitted to take a share in the mine also. In 1880, he sold his share of the Alice and bought an interest in the Anaconda Mine. He attempted to interest the Walker Brothers in this mine, but they declined. He then approached his old friend George Hearst in the spring of 1881. By this time Hearst was a member of a partnership with James Ben Ali Haggin and Lloyd Tevis, who were investing in mining. After Hearst looked at the site, he convinced his partners of the potential of the Anaconda Mine and they agreed to back its development. Daly sold them the mine for his purchase price of $30,000 ($820,000 in 2022 dollars)[14] and was allotted a 25 percent ownership. He was hired as superintendent to develop it.[15] Initially the Anaconda was a silver mine, and they used the Dexter Mill leased from W.A. Clark to extract the silver. It was a very good silver producer. However, about a year after its development a massive deposit of copper was discovered. Since the ores were of mid-grade quality it was apparent it would be too costly to ship the ore elsewhere for refinement. If the deposit was to be developed, it would be necessary to build a smelter near the mine. Daly again went to his backers and proposed a major investment to smelt the copper ore. The investment required was significantly greater than that needed for the silver mine. While demand for copper was increasing because of the recent discovery of applications of electricity for commercial use, the mine was located a long way from potential markets. In addition, Montana was noted for its long, hard winters which made travel difficult. The only access to the outside world was a newly constructed narrow-gauge railroad to Corinne, Utah, 400 miles away.[16] Daly, with the help of Haggin, finally convinced Hearst and Tevis to go along with the plan. Now that the major players were heavily involved in the Butte mines, the stage was set for the fabulous growth of mining in Butte and the huge demand for wood that went along with it.[17]

CHAPTER TWO

Early Logging and Transportation History

With the initial discovery of placer gold in the vicinity of Butte in 1864, a fledgling wood industry was born. Early demand was primarily for wood to build sluice boxes, flumes to carry water to the workings, and wood to provide heat and cook food. As camps developed, log cabins were constructed. At its peak during the placer mining period, the area may have supported as many as 5,000 people.[1] A population of this size probably used an estimated two to six thousand cords of wood during the peak year of activity. (A cord of wood is a stack of wood eight feet long, four feet high and four feet wide.) Other forest products used in the mining industry included lagging (planks or timbers used to line the mine tunnels to prevent rocks from falling in the mine shaft), stulls (timbers used to support the roof of the mine shaft), and converter poles (green poles that are added to the molten ore to reduce oxides in it).[2] Initially, wood was obtained from the forests adjacent to Butte, but it is unknown if men were employed full time in acquiring wood or if the miners were involved. The 1870 census did not list any individuals whose occupation was indicated as a woodchopper. There were two men listed as sawyers who probably operated a sawmill for lumber production.[3] By this time, however, the placer claims had been worked out and the population had dropped to 241 people in Butte City. Consequently, the demand for wood dropped substantially.[4] Mining in the Butte area remained limited until about 1874 when new milling processes were introduced that were successful in reducing silver ores, thus beginning the hard rock mining period.[5] With the introduction of these new milling methods there was a significant increase in the need for wood. In December of 1876, the *Semi-Weekly Miner* reported that "*. . . more men this season are engaged in cutting and hauling timber than has ever before been so employed. There have been large contracts for fuel for the various mills let out and the rapid growth of the town requiring heavy timbers for building purposes and supplies of cord wood for fuel has given the lumber men all they can do to meet the wants of the people and unless the season should be an open and favorable one a scarcity of this article may be anticipated before spring.*"[6] Because of the sparse timber cover near Butte, it did not take long to use up the available wood. A news article in February 1877 stated that large quantities of wood were being felled in the neighboring gulches surrounding Butte and hauled out upon sleds to storage points.[7] Wagons were used during the rest of the year. To answer the increased need for lumber, several sawmills were established near Butte. In March of 1877, a news article in the *Semi-Weekly Miner* reported that a new sawmill was being set up on the summit of the main range eighteen to twenty miles south of Butte.[8] The article also mentions that a sawmill was also working in the "Park." (This area was located north of Butte toward the town of Basin and is now referred to as Elk Park.) This mill was probably in the vicinity of present-day Woodville, which would require a haul of about eight miles to Butte. The article went on to express the opinion that a scarcity of wood is not likely to occur because of these mills. That summer the paper announced the upgrading of the sawmill on Warm Springs Creek by Mr. Brundy to increase its capacity.[9] There also was a continued demand for cordwood; however, woodcutters may have been limited. A request to supply 1,200 cords of wood in 1877 brought only three bids.[10] To compound the problem, the *Semi-Weekly Miner* reported on December 18, 1877, that Marshal W.F. Wheeler had seized all the cordwood stacked about the different mills as well as the lumber in the different sale yards.[11] After he left the city his deputy Mr. Vantleburg searched the neighboring forest and seized any cordwood he found. The problem revolved around cutting green timber on public domain. At this point in time almost all the forest land near Butte was part of the public domain and controlled by the federal government. The land was managed by the General Land Office (GLO) in the Department of Interior. While woodcutters were permitted to cut dead material there, they were required to pay for the green timber, which they were not doing. People felt that the seizures of the timber would have little effect on the mills as the federal timber lands were soon to be sold based on the many timber bills already introduced in Congress. The logger could recover his wood by paying $1.00 per cord, which the *Semi-Weekly Miner* referred to as "*exorbitant and oppressive.*"[12] The seized timber was to be put up for sale if not paid for by the logger, and the paper warned it would be extremely unhealthy for any buyer to bid on it. The paper expressed the idea that the logger should be able to buy it for a price not higher than twenty-five cents per cord. The loss of the wood supply quickly set in motion efforts at the national level to permit cutting of green material on the public domain. The *Semi-Weekly Miner* reported on April 30, 1878, that a bill had been passed on April 18th to permit cutting green timber on areas identified as mineral lands and the problem was partially resolved.[13] Land was considered mineral lands if there was the potential to mine valuable minerals there.

Figure 1 – Hauling wood for the Colorado Smelter, 1880s. Pack horses shown in the middle right of the picture were used to bring the wood down to the landing to be loaded on the wagons. Photograph courtesy of University of Montana Archives and Special Collections (74-317). Photographer unknown.

Apparently, there was no organized effort to identify mineral lands; it appears lands got the designation when a mine was developed. Cutting green timber on non-mineral land was still illegal, and this issue continued to plague the woodcutters and mining interests.

Logging increased as mining and smelting increased in the Butte area and additional sawmills were established. By the 1880 census, there were at least 217 men working as woodchoppers and at least fifty-three men hauling wood.[14] Cordwood prices varied greatly from $4 to $7 per cord, or about $117 to $205 in 2022 dollars.[15] The *Semi-Weekly Miner* reported on February 8, 1882, that in the "Park" (Elk Park) there were at least 500 men engaged in wood chopping, and many thousands of cords were already ricked or stacked along with thousands more on the ground, which would not be piled until spring or until after the snow had gone.[16]

That summer, cord wood was listed at $5.50 per cord (about $161 in 2022 dollars); by November it was listed at $7.00 per cord (about $205 in 2022 dollars).[17] In the August 5th edition of the *Semi-Weekly Miner* is listed over 56,000 cords under contract with 125 teams coming in from the "Park" every day.[18] By 1883, the Alice Mine alone was using 1,000 cords a month.[19] It is estimated that a team of horses could pull a wagon loaded with up to one and a half cords of wood during a regular work day.[20] This rate of delivery required over 666 trips just to supply the needs of the Alice Mine. With increased demand, woodcutters were required to search for wood farther from Butte, resulting in transportation issues (Figure 1). The length of the haul made it unfeasible to haul wood by wagon or sleds. Consequently, suppliers began looking for alternative methods of delivering their product to town. Thus, the stage was set for a major change in the transportation system used to supply wood to the mines and mills.

CHAPTER THREE

Flumes Arrive in Butte

It became apparent that the growing mining and smelting industry in Butte could not be supported by horses and wagons. Timber harvest had already removed most of the wood close to Butte and the distance required to haul wood from the "Park" was making wagon delivery marginal. A new method of transportation was needed.

As early as 1864, flumes were being used in Nevada and California to transport lumber or cordwood from the woods.[1] Initially these were flat bottomed and required an unlimited water supply. This type of flume also is prone to "hang-ups," especially with shorter-length material. Sometime around 1868 the first "V"-shaped flumes, which required significantly less water, made their appearance. Hang-ups were also less of a problem. By 1879 there were over eighty miles of wood and lumber flumes carrying 171,000 cords of wood and 33.3 million board feet of lumber in Nevada.[2] A flume constructed in 1875 by the Pacific Wood and Lumber Flume Company near Lake Tahoe was fifteen miles in length and could deliver 500 cords of wood per day. It would have required 2,000 horses to deliver the same amount. It was estimated that it cost $1 per cord (about $27 per cord in 2022)[3] to deliver wood with a flume. Using horses and a wagons would cost several times more.[4] It can readily be seen that a change from wagon delivery would both be cheaper and require significantly less workers and horsepower.

The first mention of flume use in the Butte area appeared in 1879 in an article in the *Semi-Weekly Miner*.[5] It stated that the owners of the Bedrock Flume were putting in a wood flume from Black Tail Canyon to the end of Main Street, a distance of about six and a half miles. No particulars were given on the type of construction. The article went on to state that wood flumes of this description are quite common in Nevada, but they thought it was the first of its kind in Montana. No further mention could be found about this operation in subsequent years. There is a brief mention of a suit against the Western Wood & Flume Co. in 1882, but it is unclear if they had constructed a flume and where it was located.[6]

In the spring of 1883, an article in the *Semi-Weekly Miner* related the story of a new flume being constructed to float cordwood from the Basin Creek Falls to the Colorado Smelter.[7] At that time about nine miles had been constructed, with water running through seven miles of it. It required trestles from twenty to seventy feet high, and it was estimated that between 800,000 to 1,000,000 board feet (bf) of lumber and 350 kegs of nails would be used in construction. (A board foot is equal to a board twelve inches long, twelve inches wide and one inch thick.) The total length was to be thirteen miles and save from $2.50 to $3 per cord (about $74 to $89 in 2022) in transportation costs.[8] Its dimensions were three feet wide at the bottom, with twenty-four-inch-inch sides. It also stated the company had acquired sufficient water rights to ensure a steady supply of water and that the expected capacity of the flume would be sufficient to deliver the wood consumed by the Colorado Smelter and probably enough to supply a large portion of the wood used by the mills and private parties in the Butte market. An article in the same paper on July 4 indicated that water had been turned into the flume, but it leaked heavily because the dry wood used in construction and material could not be floated with the present flow. It was expected that the wood would swell and the flume would become water-tight after further use.[9] The August 20, 1883, *Helena Daily Independent* indicated the flume was fourteen miles long and was expected to deliver 800 cords of wood every twelve hours doing the work of 800 two-horse teams. The leaking problem had been resolved and a pile of wood 300 feet long, 40 feet wide, and 8-10 feet high was reported to have been delivered to the mill. Seven men patrolled the flume, and the company was expected to run 150,000 cords the next year. The operation stopped for the year in September due to lack of water.[10] On October 10th of that year, it was reported that 100,000 feet of lumber, some of it heavy timbers thirty feet in length, had been floated down the Basin Flume to the Colorado Smelter.[11]

While it appears the Colorado Smelter flume was a success, a "V"-shaped flume would be more efficient for the Butte area, where water was limiting. All subsequent flumes apparently were of this design. J.C. Robinson began making plans for a flume to supply the town of Deer Lodge with firewood and other products.[12] It appears this work was also started in the spring of 1883, but there is no apparent relation between this and the Colorado Smelter Flume. Robinson's project proposed putting a sawmill in the woods and cutting the wood into whatever length the customer wanted and then floating it to the edge of town, where it could be delivered to individual users. The flume was to be seven miles long and run from the headwaters of Tin Cup Joe Creek to the edge of Deer Lodge. It was "V"-shaped with eighteen-inch sides and used about 200 inches of water. Robinson set up a sawmill at the head of the flume with a capacity of five to six thousand board feet per day and powered by a 10-inch horizontal Leffel turbine. It was estimated that 175,000 board feet of lumber was required for the flume and would cost eight to ten thousand dollars ($236,000 to $295,100 in 2022).[13] Seven men were employed, and the number was expected to increase as the business demands increased. It was anticipated that the flume would be completed and wood dropped at the exit of the flume in August 1883. Follow-up reports suggested that construction did not proceed as quickly as had been predicted, and in October of that year the flume was still two miles from town, reaching Roulean's Field. The sawmill produced stove wood, cordwood, and lumber, and the owners stated they would also do such custom work as the market demanded.[14] It was not until August of the following year, however, that the newspaper reported that the flume was completed. Its terminus was west of the brewery and the flume was about eight miles long. The capacity of the flume was to be 100 cords a day, but because of the limited production of the sawmill, the capacity was less than half that amount. The quoted price for firewood was $5 ($152 in 2022) per cord delivered in any length.[15] The *Weekly Anaconda Review* later reported that the flume was completed to the railroad dump on Tin Cup Joe Creek at the cost of $12,000 ($365,920 in 2022) and had a capacity of thirty cords a day.[16]

Other flumes soon were being mentioned in the newspapers of the day. The *Semi-Weekly Miner* announced a court case against the Western Wood & Flume Company or Transportation Company. There is no indication where the flume was located or even if there was a flume, as the name changed between the two articles.[17]

A flume in German Gulch later referred to as the Williams Flume caused a stir and hard feelings in 1886. A trio of landowners (Thomas Ford, Charles Carver, and James Larkin) felt that Henry Williams and Atkin Smith had built a wood flume across their land without their permission. They decided to correct the problem by tearing it down. Williams and Smith claimed that the flume was over 300 feet from the ground of the trio and signed a complaint against the landowners. A party of three or four officers went to German Gulch and arrested the landowners, bringing them back to Butte, where they were arraigned before Judge Lippincett with bail set at $500. No references were found indicating the results of the trial. Subsequent stories in the newspapers indicated that the flume was repaired and operated at least through 1887.[18]

This flume was involved with another major problem in the fall of 1886. A person or persons unknown set the wood that was piled by the railroad at the base of the flume on fire, causing the loss of an estimated 33,000 cords of wood. The fire also burned ten freight cars that were adjacent to the woodpile. The heat was so great that it warped the rails of the track, and all trains were stopped for twelve hours. The loss was estimated at $4,000 (almost $126,800 in 2022) to the railroad and about $100,000 ($3,170,000 in 2022) for the lost wood.[19] Insurance only covered half of the wood loss. A reward of $4,000 ($126,800 in 2022) was offered for the arrest and conviction of those who committed the act.[20] No suspect was ever found. (Could the fire have been set by the landowners in retaliation for their arrest?) Apparently, the damage was repaired, and the *Semi-Weekly Miner* indicated that operations would resume, as they had a good head of water and they expected to bring down several hundred cords of wood per day.[21]

The Jerry Creek Flume located in Silver Bow Canyon also burned in the fall of 1886. The *Semi-Weekly Miner* reported that the company had been paid $48,750 by their insurance company for the wood that was lost.[22] The paper also indicated that their tax had been reduced from $50,000 to $40,000.[23] That fall the company filed its annual report, which showed a capital stock value of $150,000 and a debt of $65,000.[24]

The Willow Creek Fluming Company was organized in 1894 to log the Willow Creek Drainage. This flume will be discussed in Chapter 11.

And finally, in 1895, there is mention of flume activity with a notice in the *Anaconda Standard* about a lawsuit concerning the Lowland Flume Company owned by Branagan and Fred Caplice.[25] Use of flumes continued well into the 1900s; they were slowly replaced by trucks thereafter.

As you can see, by the time Marcus Daly began developing the Anaconda Company Smelter in 1883, logging flumes were well in use in the area as a means of transporting material from the woods to the mill or town site. They soon became even more widely used; without doubt, the most important flume constructed for the Butte-Anaconda area was started that year to provide lumber for the Anaconda townsite and later was used by Caplice and McCune to provide cordwood for the Anaconda operation.

CHAPTER FOUR

Public Domain and Timber Cutting

Prior to the discovery of valuable minerals in Montana, all land was originally public domain owned by the federal government with the exception of those lands set aside as reservations for the Indian Nations or given to the state as school trust lands.[1] When a miner located a mineral claim, there were procedures in place for him to acquire the right to mine the mineral and potentially gain ownership of the ground. There were, however, limited legal ways that he could obtain wood for use in development of the mine. This law did not stop people from taking timber from these lands, as the attitude of the public at the time was that the public domain was open to everyone and the resources were free for the taking. With this mindset, logging was actively pursued on the public domain. By the late 1800s there was a push by the conservationists of the time to put the timbered public domain lands into forest reserves and protect them from illegal cutting. Under this change, no timber could be removed from a forest reserve unless it was classified as mineral lands—and then, only dead timber could be removed. Mineral lands contained a mineral underneath the surface that could be removed and sold. This restriction to remove only dead timber from mineral lands was widely ignored and cutting continued on the forests near Butte to support the development of the mines. This problem came to a head in 1877, when cutting of green material on public land was stopped by the federal government (Chapter 2). Pressure was immediately applied on Congress by the mining interests to remedy the situation. While a few operations were halted by the actions of the federal officers, cutting generally continued as before. The *Semi-Weekly Miner* reported: "*From the amount of lumber sent to Butte by the Willow Creek Lumber Co. one would almost think the U.S. Marshals had never been invented.*"[2]

Finally, on April 18, 1878, the Senate passed a bill authorizing bona fide residents in nine western states to cut any timber growing on mineral lands for building, agricultural, mining, or other domestic purposes.[3] While this law finally provided a way to obtain necessary wood for development, enforcement was lax and, in most cases, there was no evaluation of the area's mineral content, nor if the wood was to be used for domestic purposes. To further complicate the issue, land was given to the railroads to help pay for their construction. These lands represented alternate sections along the railroad right-of-way, creating a checkerboard pattern on the landscape. The original legislation authorizing this bill was signed by President Lincoln in 1864, but it would take decades before much of this land was surveyed. Consequently, there was no way to ensure that the logging supposedly occurring on railroad lands was in fact on railroad lands. In addition, uncertainty toward how the law was being enforced continued to concern woodcutters. The meaning of the words "for domestic purposes" resulted in varying enforcement of the law. Finally, in May of 1882, Secretary of the Interior Henry Teller defined the term to mean that anyone may cut timber on public lands and sell it to miners and mill operators and be considered as woodcutting for domestic purposes. It still required the land to be considered mineral lands, and the timber cut had to meet certain size requirements.[4]

While changes in the law provided some control of the handling of the public lands, enforcement of the rules continued to be lax. The number of investigators was limited, and they were required to cover large areas. Furthermore, they were faced with a hostile population. For some investigators it provided an opportunity to make some extra money by ignoring what was occurring on the ground.[5] In addition, conflicts between the woodchoppers themselves was a constant problem. One example occurred near Butte in which a group of white men took over the operation worked by a group of forty Chinese. The *Semi-Weekly Miner* reported that constable "Cap" Owen went to the work site, arrested six men, and brought them to town. Mr. Chance Harris was charged as the ringleader of the group, and they were all charged with interfering with the rights of the Chinese, who had a contract to cut wood for the Colorado Smelter.[6] No follow-up article was found relating to the trial for the six men or the outcome of the case.

Mining and milling of silver ore was in full swing in Butte by 1882 and numerous groups were cutting wood around the town. In the area known as Elk Park, or the "Park" north of Butte, an estimated 500 men were cutting. This activity was ongoing, with no concern that the area was public domain and probably did not qualify as mineral land. A letter to the editor in the *Semi-Weekly Miner* states: "*The wood choppers of Silver Bow County are deserving of great credit for the enterprise they have shown. Nothing seems to daunt them in their work - work which must be done in order that our great mining interests may not be stinted, work which is absolutely necessary and most decidedly beneficial to the interests of the camp at large.*"[7]

Efforts made by the federal government to control the illegal cutting were met with strong responses in the press. An article in the *Semi-Weekly Miner* represents the strong feeling at the local level. It states about a seizure of wood by one of the Federal Marshals: *"It is one of the characteristics of carpet-bag officials that they look out for "number one" regardless of the interests of the people. They are here to make money. They do not consider it home. They know that they secure their positions without regard to the sentiment of the people of the Territories and in defiance of such sentiment, and hence they naturally care but little for popular opinion."*[8]

With the arrival of the Northern Pacific Railroad a whole new market was opened for the timber found along the right of way. The Montana Improvement Company was incorporated by Edward L. Bonner, Richard A. Eddy, Andrew B. Hammond, and Washington Dunn to cut timber on the railroad sections and at the same time preserve the forests from wasteful cutting and fires.[9] The news article in the *New Northwest* states: *"The eight mills recently employed in sawing ties, timbers, etc., for the construction of the N.P. road, are already at work cutting lumber for this enterprise. They have already about six million feet cut, stacked, and seasoning, and are adding to the quantity 250,000 feet* (bf) *a day. About 175 to 200 men will be employed by the company."* While the company was authorized to harvest timber from the railroad sections, most of the land had not been surveyed. As late as 1903 most of the area was still unsurveyed, so it was not possible to determine what land they owned.[10] Consequently, harvest may have occurred where the best timber was found, and, by removing all the volume from the area, they could meet the company's objective of reducing the risk of a fire destroying any valuable timber.

Such were the conditions around Butte regarding use of the public domain lands when Marcus Daly went into large-scale copper mining. Not only did the business community feel they had a right to the free use of public domain timber, but the citizens themselves felt much the same, for without an available source of wood there would be few jobs to be had. It probably was only natural that Daly would look to the public domain to supply his wood needs without too much concern about paying for the wood.

CHAPTER FIVE

Early History of the Anaconda Company

With the discovery of the copper lode and the decision to develop it, Marcus Daly was faced with several major decisions to get the project off the ground. First it was decided that the ores he found could not be economically processed with the present smelters in Butte. The works in Baltimore, Maryland, or Swansea, Wales, offered better facilities, but freight to these points would make the operation uneconomical. For this reason, it was decided to erect new smelting works in or near Butte, which brought Daly to his second major decision: where it should be located. To prevent speculators from determining where the new smelter was to be located and thus prevent Daly from buying up the land at a reasonable price, he quietly began taking options on land at three different locations. It can be imagined what was going on in the business world of Butte. Knowing where the mill was to be built, how large an installation was proposed, and when it was expected to be completed were important issues. The business that guessed correctly could be guaranteed a fortune in profits. Meanwhile, Daly's men quietly evaluated several sites in the area. While Butte would have been a natural choice because of the proximity to the mines, it had major disadvantages, including the lack of suitable fluxes such as limestone, silica, and others, which are added in the smelting of ores to remove impurities. It also had a scarcity of wood for fuel and, more importantly, an unreliable supply of water. The mouth of the Blackfoot River and lower Warm Spring Creek were examined, but while they had a good water supply, the available grounds were limited and the hauling distance from Butte was too long. The Big Hole Valley was also considered. There was plenty of cheap land, water, and timber, but it required hauling the ores across the Continental Divide. Meanwhile, there was a constant hounding by people in the know to find out details about the final location.[1] The *Semi-Weekly Miner* reports one such exchange: *"If the Anaconda Company busts up next summer and ain't able to pay their debts, then the public will have a right to know all about our business; but just now it's none of their d-d business."*[2] The article goes on to state that once the ore bodies are uncovered, the copper ore will have to be smelted in the area; that, looking forward to such a contingency, the company had purchased or bonded three pieces of property, any one of which would be an eligible site for a smelter, but it is not known which one they will build on. In February 1883, the *New Northwest* paper reported that the Anaconda Company had bonded a tract of land in the Big Hole for one year for $1,000.[3] Meanwhile, Daly had decided that the upper Warm Springs Creek area best fit his needs as it had available land, a good supply of water plus deposits of limestone and iron ore in the vicinity, a short haul for ores, and accessibility to both the Union Pacific and Northern Pacific railroads.[4]

The *New Norwest* reported that Daly had Morgan Evans discreetly begin buying land with the direction to "*Pay every man whose farm you wish and who wishes to sell a liberal price therefore.*"[5] He was able to acquire for the company some 3,000 acres of land at a cost of over $30,000 (about $885,300 in 2022 dollars) before word leaked out in the press of the proposed site for the smelter.[6] The article also describes the location of the new smelter and explained that the works could be located on ten acres of ground, but since the fumes from the smelters would destroy all vegetation in their immediate vicinity within a few years, the company bought the cultivable land that may be injured so no damage could occur to any other persons by reason of the smelters. It was also proposed to dump all the tailings on lands bought for that purpose so that they would not injure farms downstream. (Unfortunately, these perceptions were untrue, and numerous lawsuits were brought against the company. Eventually the site became a Superfund site in the 1990s to repair the damage.) They expected the smelter to be working by the first of October 1883 with a capacity of smelting 300 tons per day. The article suggests that over a million board feet of lumber would be required, plus 50,000 fire bricks and 500,000 common bricks for construction.[7] Daly expected to use coal in the smelter, but this use was delayed, as there was no main rail line into Butte and the Montana coal mines were just being developed. By 1886, however, coal use had slowly increased, with the smelter using 180 tons of coal and 125 cords of wood a day.[8] It was estimated the works would cost about $500,000 ($14,755,000 in 2022 dollars) and employ over 200 men.[9] A railroad was to be constructed from the mines in Butte to the mill in upper Warm Springs Creek and a town built at the mill site.

Once the location of the smelter was announced there was a steady string of articles in the newspapers of the state describing the activity in the proposed mill site. The *New Northwest* reported in June 1883 that a ditch to bring water to the mill site was almost complete, with eighty men employed in its construction. Water rights for Warms Spring Creek were obtained from Alex and Mary Glover in March of that year.[10] Surveys were underway for the railroad and the new town of Copperopolis (shortly after renamed to Anaconda) was also being surveyed. Ross Clark had begun building a general merchandise store and there were two canvas-covered boarding houses, one with sleeping bunks on each side to accommodate forty men and many tents strung along the creek. Two brickyards were also being built to fill a contract for 500,000 bricks. Two companies providing four-horse stage transportation between Butte and Anaconda were established, both going the same day and returning the next. By June 1883, there were eight saloons, six boarding houses, two clothing and variety shops, and two blacksmith shops in the new town of Anaconda.[11] In July, the company purchased the Brundy mill site with two ditches and water rights on Mill Creek along with an interest in the road. This sawmill soon became important for providing lumber for construction in Anaconda.[12] Lots were selling for $500 to $750 ($14,755 to $22,133 in 2022 dollars) in the town site.[13] Other water rights were acquired for North and South Mill Creek and main Mill Creek in July 1883.[14] By August there were 400 men working in the camp and thirty buildings were under contract.[15] In addition, there were 125 graders leveling over an acre of ground for the mill site and about eighty houses were being built including seven hotels and boarding houses, twelve saloons, and six stores.[16] The paper also stated: "*The rumors which were spread that the whole enterprise was a swindle and that the company did not intend to go to work were laid at rest on the morning of the 23d by the commencement of the work of excavating for the smelter and concentrating works, and now the hillside chosen for their location bears a strong resemblance to a beehive, about a hundred men being employed in and around it."*[17] By October, a total of 2,700,000 bricks had been made at Anaconda for the smelter and town buildings.[18] In March of 1884 it was reported that 500 people lived in Anaconda, and it was expected to increase to 1,500–2,000 permanent residents.[19] By April 1884, the railroad grading between Anaconda and Butte was progressing rapidly with four grading camps on the line. There were approximately seventy-five men and twenty-five teams of horses at each camp for a total of 300 men and 100 teams doing the grading.[20] Finally, the September 12th, 1884, *New Northwest* reported that the first fire was started in the furnaces and smelting would begin after the expenditure of nearly $4,000,000 (about $121,640,000 in 2022 dollars) for mining development, machinery, and buildings.[21]

The completion of the plant heralded the beginning of the huge increase in the demand for wood products to fuel the smelters and supply the needs of the new town. With this demand came the need for a form of cheap transportation to deliver the material to where it was needed and thus began one of the largest systems of flumes in the state to support this undertaking.

CHAPTER SIX

The First Timber Contract

As the completion of the mill located in Anaconda approached, Marcus Daly turned his attention to obtaining a supply of fuel for its operation. During this time steam power from coal or wood-fired boilers was the principal power source for most all western mining operations. Unfortunately, there were no coal deposits near the Butte area, the closest mines being near Bozeman and Gardiner, Montana. Because of the distance from Butte, a railroad was required to make the delivery. The Utah & Northern Railroad (U&N) built a narrow-gauge railroad into Butte from Brigham City, Utah, in 1881, but it did not connect with any of the coalfields. Completion of the Northern Pacific Railroad (NP) line to Garrison, Montana, did not occur until September of 1883. An agreement between NP and U&N prevented the NP from building into Butte and consequently the use of coal from Bozeman or Gardiner would require hauling the coal past Butte to Garrison to be loaded on cars that could run on the narrow-gauge track back to Butte.[1] Apparently this was not a feasible approach, and at least for the short-term Daly had no alternative but to use the seemingly unlimited supply of wood immediately adjacent to Anaconda. That the wood was located on the public domain did not deter developers of the time from taking their share. Most people viewed the timber as a resource that should be available to use to "develop the country" and thought that whoever got there first could take it.

David Neagle had the first contract with Daly to provide wood for the Anaconda operation. Neagle was born in Boston on October 10, 1847.[2] He grew up in the San Francisco Bay area, where he earned a reputation for being a handy man with a gun while roaming through the mining camps of the west. At various times he was a gambler, politician, saloonkeeper, and lawman. During the height of the Earp-Clanton feud in 1880, Neagle served as deputy sheriff of Tombstone, Arizona. While there, he shot a Mexican in the back with a rifle. He was also accused of shooting at James Levy, a miner, in Nevada.[3] Apparently, no charges were brought against Neagle for either of these actions. He was unbiased in his dealings with both the Earps and Clantons and, as a result, was elected as city marshal in Tombstone in January 1882. His later attempt to become sheriff failed, however, and he eventually moved to Montana in 1883.[4] He became a foreman for Daly, in charge of a gang that was grading the area for the smelter. Upon completion of this work, Daly instructed him to take his crew up Mill Creek and cut wood for the smelter. This he did in the winter of 1883.[5] He had an oral contract with Daly to cut 30,000 cords of wood at $2.25 per cord. He also got $.60 per cord for banking and fluming the wood. (Banking referred to the wood being stacked in piles from which it could be transported to the user.) He was to deliver 16,000 cords to the mill in the spring by a flume which was to be constructed. This was undertaken by D.

A. Spaker of Anaconda.[6] John Hay had the contract to bank and flume the wood for delivery during the summer of 1884. Neagle employed several woodcutters, who spent the winter cutting wood. They lived in small cabins where they worked. There is no record where his crew worked, but it probably was in Mill Creek or Clear Creek. Apparently, the standard practice for the woodcutters was to cut the wood in the winter—making stacks where it was cut—and then another group of men would haul it to the flume and bank it until it could be floated down to the wood yard. The fluming season generally started in May and ran to November. Since the wood was not scaled until it reached the mill, the workers were not paid until after the wood reached the "dump" at the end of the flume. Here the wood was scaled, and the woodcutters were paid. Since it was a year between paydays for the cutters, some arrangement had to be made to provide them with credit to purchase supplies for subsistence during the rest of the year. Consequently, they were given credit at the company store based on an estimate of the wood cut but not yet delivered to the wood yard.[7]

Neagle apparently was not too keen on the idea of living in a drafty cabin on the job, so he elected to live in town with his family and make visits to the camp two or three times a week. He would get on his horse, ride out to the work area, and check on the progress of the cutters. Based on these visits and his observations, he would authorize various amounts of credit for his cutters at the company store run by Mr. Estes. It did not take long for the woodcutters to realize that the deep snows could be used to their advantage to "enhance" the size of their cuttings, and by judicious rearrangement of the snow and piling of wood they had cut they were able to markedly increase their output and subsequently their credit at the store. Thus passed a pleasant winter for the woodcutters, who lived high while minimizing the amount of physical work, and for Neagle, who had the comforts of home and social life of the city.

As spring approached and it became time to bank up the wood by the flume, one after another of the woodcutters "rolled his blankets" and left the camp without measuring his wood or waiting for a settlement. It was obvious to them that as the snow melted in the stacks, they may come up a "little short." Every trip Neagle made to the camp showed fewer men and more empty cabins. He knew something was going on and had a good idea what it was. Not being the mildest tempered man, he became highly agitated about the affairs at the camp. One day, while riding to camp, he met one of his woodcutters named David Maginnis coming down the trail with his blanket on his back. He became terribly angry and ordered the man back to camp. When he declined, Neagle drew his pistol and shot the woodcutter. Later, Neagle said Maginnis had a knife in his hand. He then returned to town and turned himself in to Justice of Peace Edwin Waterbury. Neagle was put in jail and Justice Waterbury rode out to the scene of the shooting. On the way he met a party bringing in the wounded man, who had not died after all. He was put up at the Grand Central Hotel at Neagle's expense and subsequently recovered. Neagle was held on $5,000 bail and bound over to the district court. He put up the bail and was released. On May 1, 1885, an article appeared in the *New Northwest* newspaper that stated Neagle's case was number 1992—assault with a deadly weapon—to which Neagle pleaded not guilty. The trial was set for May 6, 1885, and bail was reduced to $1,500. Finally, on December 11, 1885, an item in the *New Northwest* stated that by a motion of the District Attorney for a *nolle pros* (plaintiff is unwilling to pursue) the case was dropped. We can speculate as to why the case was dropped; it could be that some money changed hands and the woodcutter left for healthier parts. After the shooting Neagle never visited his woodworkers' camp alone.[8]

Neagle apparently continued working with his crew that summer to flume the wood they had cut to the mill in Anaconda. The records indicate that he supplied about 12,000 cords, which was not sufficient to meet Daly's needs.[9] Daly was not happy with his work, so he paid him $1,000 to terminate their agreement.[10] Thus ended Neagle's wood cutting days.

In August of 1884, a story appeared in the *Arizona Daily Star* concerning Dave Neagle.[11] It stated he was a well-known resident of Tombstone and had murdered a man in Montana. The story came from Judge Murphy that Neagle and the man he killed were partners in a mine in Butte. Neagle's partner supposedly drew $600 from the mine's assets to pay the men employed there, but he instead skipped town with the money. Neagle found out about it and chased after the man. When he caught up to him his partner began shooting at Neagle. Neagle returned fire and killed his partner with the first shot. He retrieved the money and subsequently paid his employees. He was honorably discharged by a magistrate and became very popular with the miners. He supposedly had a position in the sheriff's office and was a popular candidate for that position in the coming election. No story supporting this event could be found in the Montana press. It could represent a variation of his shooting of the woodchopper.

He returned to San Francisco in 1885 and became deputy sheriff. In 1888 he was appointed deputy United States Marshall. He shot and killed Judge David Terry in 1889 but, through some questionable legal maneuvering, was acquitted of the charge of murder. He continued to live in the San Francisco area and was embroiled in various confrontations over the years. He died there on November 28, 1925, at the age of 78.[12]

CHAPTER SEVEN

Daly's Quandary

After the failure of Neagle's operation to provide the needed fuelwood, Marcus Daly decided to let a contract to supply the mill with 300,000 cords of wood over a four-year period. This announcement caused quite a stir in the local newspapers. One paper reported the proposal and then stated: "*Great Caesar! We wonder if they have stopped to think that at $5 per cord that will cost a million and a half of dollars.*"[1] Another paper made the analogy that if the cords were laid end-to-end they would extend 548 miles and a fraction.[2] On December 24, 1884, the *Semi-Weekly Miner* reported that the contract for furnishing the Anaconda Company with 300,000 cords of wood was signed on December 23rd by John Caplice and Alfred W. McCune.[3] (A draft agreement written by Mr. Dixon indicates the date was December 19, 1884.)[4] They contracted to deliver 75,000 cords yearly for four years. The partnership of Caplice and McCune had been active in the Butte area since 1882 or 1883 with various contracts for wood and railroad construction. This was possibly the largest contract for wood ever taken or contracted for.[5]

John Caplice first came to Butte in 1878.[6] He was born in Ireland in 1829. The eldest of three children, he was raised by his grandparents after his parents died. At twelve years of age he went out on his own, and in 1850 he immigrated to the United States. He engaged in farming for a while in Pennsylvania and Illinois. He then moved to Iowa and mined coal until 1856, then moved to Missouri and conducted a freight business on the Mississippi River in addition to woodcutting for the riverboats. At the outbreak of the Civil War, he lost the wood he had banked along the river, so he went into freighting in Denver. With the discovery of gold in Alder Gulch, he took a load of merchandise to Bannack, which provided the capital to set up his merchandising and mining ventures in Montana. He opened stores in Philipsburg and Missoula, Montana, as well as in today's ghost towns of Emmetsburg (located in Henderson Gulch between Maxville and Hall, Montana); McClellan (near Lincoln, Montana); and Forest City in Cedar Creek (near Superior, Montana). In Forest City he was partnered with a man named Smith. In July of 1872, $4,000 in gold was stolen from their store and a group of Chinese miners were blamed for the theft. Ed Warren and Pat McGrath recovered the gold twenty miles east of the Cataldo Mission (which is in present-day Idaho near Exit 39 off Interstate 90) but insisted that the Chinese had escaped. Nevertheless, rumors persisted that Warren and McGrath had murdered them.[7] Ground sluicing began in Forest City in the summer of 1873 with the construction of the Forest City Flume, of which John Caplice was listed as one of the owners.[8] Finally, in 1878, John moved to Butte and was instrumental in bringing the Union Pacific Railroad into the town. He also got into the wood business with a contract with the Walker

Brothers.[9] In addition to his wood business, the *Semi-Weekly Miner* reported that John Caplice & Co. had one of the most extensive retail stores in Butte.[10]

Alfred W. McCune began contracting work in Butte in about 1882 and moved there in 1885. He was born in Calcutta, India, on June 11, 1849, while his father was serving in the British Army.[11] He was one of seven sons. There was also a McCune daughter who died in infancy. In the 1850s, the family converted to the Mormon faith and, in 1856, his father resigned his commission, left Calcutta, and came to the United States, eventually arriving in Salt Lake, Utah, in the fall of 1857. The McCunes settled in Nephi, Utah, where they bought a farm. Alfred's first job was sheep herding. At age 19 he got his first railroad job working on the construction of the Union Pacific Railroad. He then went into the cattle business with his brother, Edward. When the Utah Southern Railroad began construction, Alfred became involved in running a grain car, which supplied hay and grain and provisions to the railroad workers. Later he took partners Joel Groves and Walter P. Read and built the railroad between Milford and Frisco, Utah. The group also had a general store in Milford. In the fall of 1879, Alfred engaged in building railroads in Colorado with his partners. They worked on the Rio Grande Railroad (RGR), the Denver and South Park Railroad (DSPR), and the Denver and New Orleans Railroad (DNOR). By 1882, their interests had moved to Idaho, where they built twenty miles of the Oregon Short Line (OSLR) west of American Falls, Idaho. At the same time, they took a contract to provide firewood to the Lexington Mine in Butte, Montana. Partly because of the firewood contract, the partnership with Groves and Read dissolved. Sometime between 1882 and late 1883 McCune and Caplice formed their partnership. Their first contract was not for wood. The *New Northwest* reported on November 16, 1883, that the Montana Railroad Company had secured the contract for building the Anaconda branch of the Utah & Northern Railroad from Stuart, Montana, to Anaconda, a distance of about eight or nine miles. The paper reported that *"Messer's. Caplice and McCune have taken the contract to do the grading and will begin the work at once. McCune is an old contractor on the Oregon Short Line where he has already a force of men whom he will bring to Stuart within a few days and the work will be pushed rapidly ahead."*[12] Later, in December, the *Semi-Weekly Miner* reported that Caplice, McCune & Co. had taken the contract to build the Utah & Northern track to the Anaconda Mine.[13] By April 1884, it was reported that they had 175 men working on the line and expected it should be ready for ties by mid-May.[14]

The business was well-established by 1884, with their ad appearing in the Montana Advertising Directory. There is evidence that the partnership was filling firewood contracts for other operations in the area prior to their contract with Daly. In a newspaper article dated February 27, 1884, the company defended its contract with the Alice Mining Company against the accusation that the price of $7 per cord was excessive. This contract called for the delivery of 15,000 cords, but no dates were indicated.[15] Finally, on December 23, 1884, they signed the contract with Daly to deliver 300,000 cords of firewood for $3.49 per cord.[16]

By this time, the economic impact of the use of firewood in Butte and Anaconda was significant—as shown by an article in the *New Northwest.* It states that the amount of wood consumed in Butte by the various mining, milling, and smelting enterprises, plus what is used by supporting business and private families, amounted to about 20,000 cords per month and provided employment for about 2,000 woodchoppers.[17] In July 1885, it was reported that the payroll for the railroad and wood camps amounted to $7,000 (about $215,040 in 2022 dollars).[18] Because flumes could not be used during the winter period, mule- and horse-drawn sleds were used to bring wood to town from closer operations. During the winter of 1884, 150 teams were used to haul wood to Walkerville daily, and as a result, it was reported that the snow was worn out on the main roads. New snow was needed, and if it did not fall soon enough, hauling would likely need to be suspended.[19] Apparently more snow arrived, and in March about 100 teams were hauling wood from the "Park," with as many as 100 more hauling from the nearby hills and camps.[20] Most of this cutting was ongoing before Caplice and McCune started their operation in Mill Creek. Their operation would add about 5,000 cords to the monthly total.

CHAPTER EIGHT

Early Operations of Caplice and McCune

To develop the smelter in Anaconda, it was necessary to acquire water rights and a right-of-way up Mill Creek so that wood cut there could be flumed to the smelter. On July 9, 1883, the company acquired water rights from the North Fork of Mill Creek (Clear Creek?), South Fork of Mill Creek, and main Mill Creek, along with the necessary right-of-way for the flume.[1] A flume was then constructed on this right of way by D.A. Spaker during the spring of 1884. It extended from the Anaconda branch of the Utah & Northern Railroad to about one-half mile above the junction of the North Fork of Mill Creek and main Mill Creek[2] (Map 1). Neagle used this flume to deliver the wood that his crew had cut during the winter of 1883–4.

When Caplice and McCune began their contract, they acquired use of this portion of flume, which was referred to as the "Smelting Company's Flume." To provide the quantity of wood the contract required, a significant increase in the work force and expansion in the cutting area was needed; hence, the flume needed to be extended. This task was undertaken by J.A. Gibson along with partners James McLeod and McDonald in 1885. They extended the flume to the Continental Divide and constructed a secondary flume up Clear Creek for three miles.[3] The record does not indicate when the flume up main Mill Creek was constructed, but it probably was part of this construction period (Maps 1 & 2). Construction of the flume was done by workmen hired or contracted to do the job rather than the regular wood cutters. Once it was decided where the logging would occur, a survey crew was sent out to locate the path of the flume. This survey determined where excavation was necessary and where the flume required support by trestles to maintain a constant grade. While most of the areas logged by Caplice and McCune was stocked with lodgepole pine and some whitebark pine, there were also some patches of Douglas fir on the dry ridges and spruce along the larger streams. These patches of larger trees were ideal for making boards for the flume.

Construction of the flume progressed in a leap-frog manner. A small sawmill powered by a wood-fired steam engine would be hauled to a site along the path of the proposed flume and set up in or near one of these stands of larger trees, where water could be added to the flume from a nearby stream. Construction on the flume would start at this point and, as the work progressed, wood from the mill would be floated down the flume or hauled by wagon to where it was needed. Once the newly built flume tied into the existing portion of the flume, the sawmill would be moved further along the proposed route and the

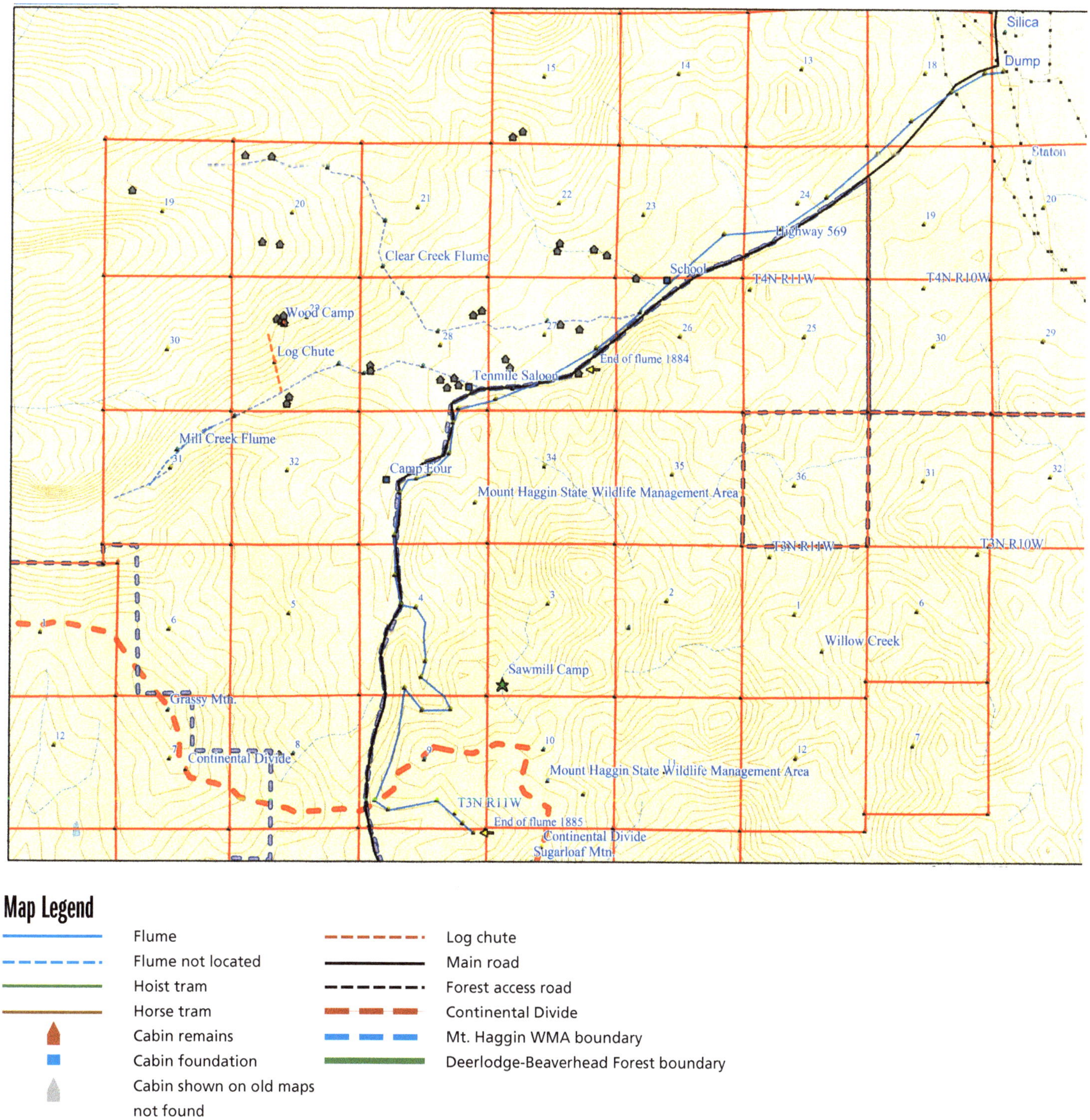

Map 1 – Map of the original McCune Flume between the "Dump" and the Continental Divide.

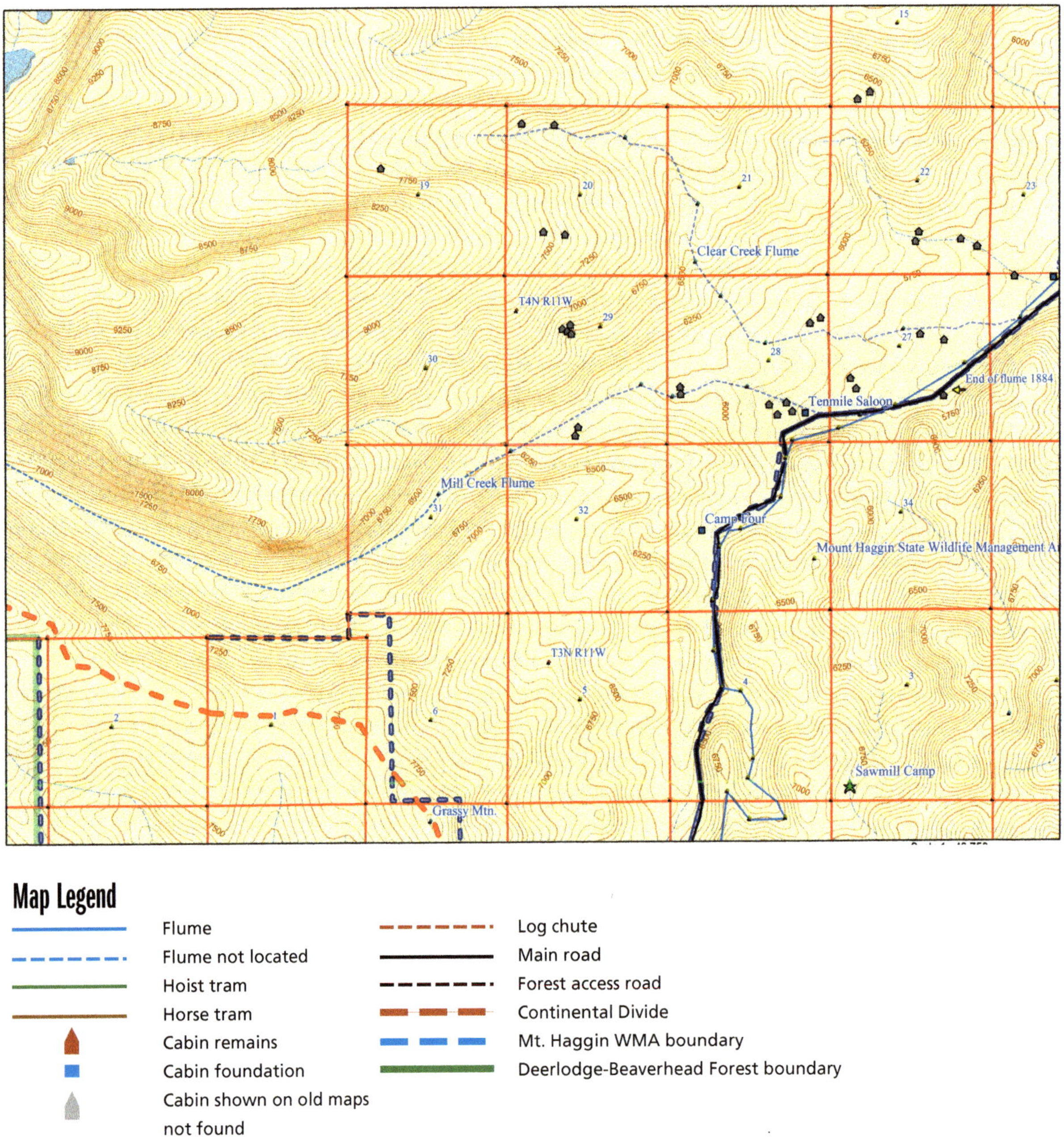

Map 2 – Map of Clear Creek and Mill Creek Flumes. Blue dashed lines represent flumes shown on Vogel's map.[4]

process would be repeated. This leap-frog method of construction continued until the "back end" of the flume was reached.[5] Apparently, the amount of timber suitable for lumber was limited and, in some cases, the sawmill was set up at a distance from the flume and the lumber was transported by wagon. Trestles were used to cross low spots and extensive excavation was done to maintain the grade of the flume. Grades varied between one-half to twelve percent. Ordinarily lower grades were avoided, as the wood was more likely to get jammed and cause a break in the flume.

The flume was constructed in a "V" shape using 1.5-inch-thick boards. The main flume was forty-two inches wide at the top with thirty-four-inch sides (Figure 2). Supports were placed every ten feet. Secondary flumes like the one on Tenmile Creek were smaller—about twenty-five inches wide with eighteen-inch

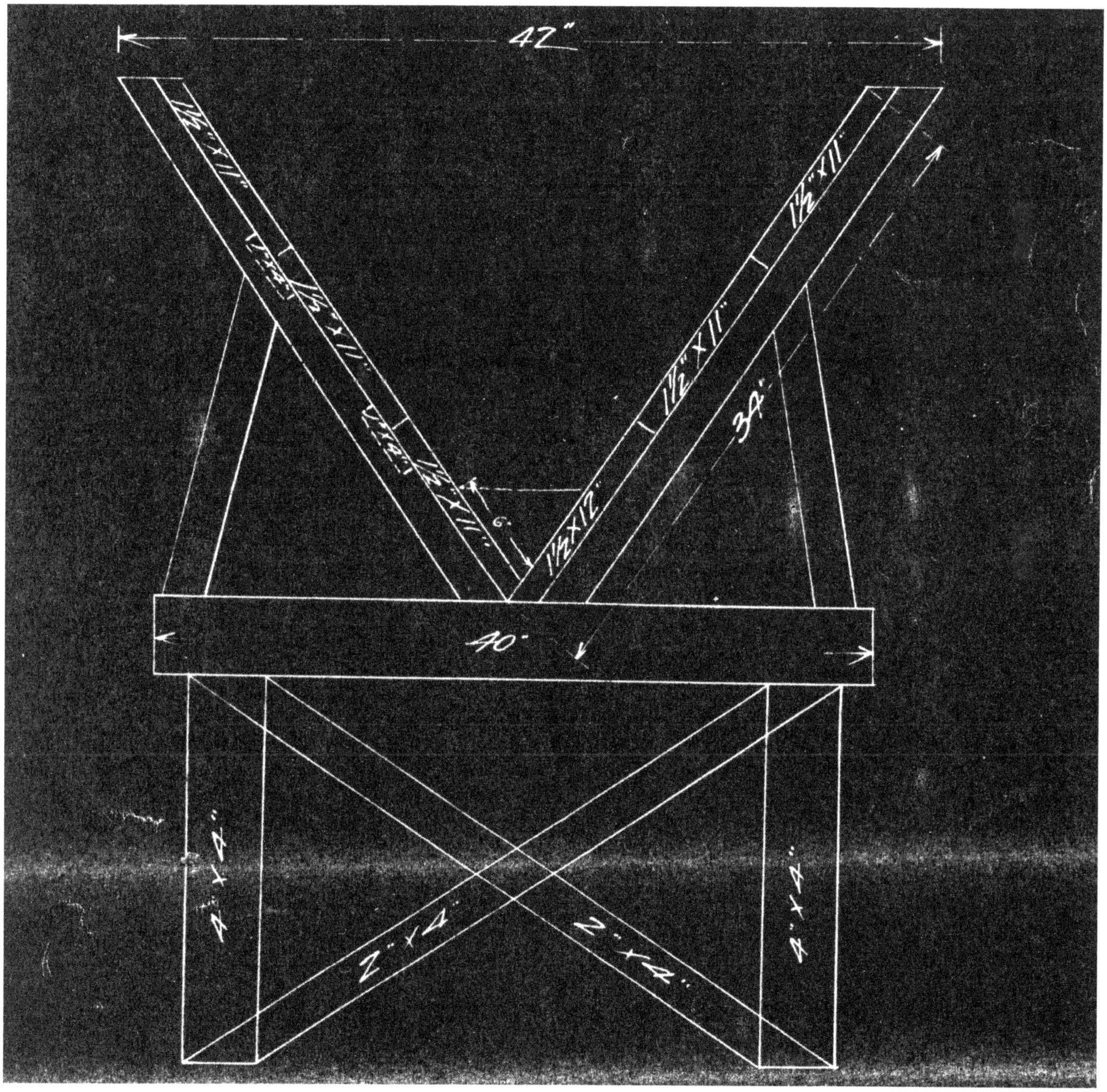

Figure 2 – Typical flume construction. From *Report to District Forester on data obtained on the Allen Flume near Anaconda, Montana, and on the Rochet Flume near St. Joe, Idaho*, by E.W. Kramer, 1912.

sides. Where the flume was elevated on a trestle, a catwalk was built along one side to permit the flume walker access for inspection and maintenance of the flume.

The braces and framing for the flume were prefabbed at the mill site and carried by wagon to where needed (Figure 3). Some of the bracing used in the trestles was slab wood from the sawmill. Construction of the flume required a great deal of hand work. Trestles were built on site and lifted into place with the help of horses. Excavation was done with a horse-drawn scraper. These were referred to as a slip, fresno, or drag scoop (Figure 4). In some cases, a horse drawn plow was used to break the ground and the slip used to remove the loosened soil.

Figure 3 – Stack of prefab flume supports found in 1998 on Tenmile Creek. These were put together at the sawmill and then transported by wagon to the point where they were used. These were apparently not needed in the flume construction in Tenmile Creek. PHOTOGRAPH BY B. JOHN LOSENSKY.

Figure 4 – Slip used to excavate path for flume located at the base of the Crooked John Tram, 2004. This simple device is pulled by a horse. Wooden control handles were attached to the brackets on the side and were used to control the depth of the cut by pushing down or lifting up on them. PHOTOGRAPH BY B. JOHN LOSENSKY.

Figure 5 – Trestle construction using manpower and horses, ca. 1905. Each section of supports was assembled and placed in its position on the ground or on the previous tier. It was then raised, and braces were added to tie it to the previous section. These supports can be seen in the photograph situated along the first tier and on the ground ready to be raised. PHOTOGRAPH COURTESY OF NATIONAL ARCHIVES RG-95-53926. PHOTOGRAPHER UNKNOWN.

This work was assisted by men with shovels.[6] Not only did the building crew need to maintain a consistent grade with no sags in the flume—they also needed to build curves in the structure to follow the topography. The spread of the trestle legs varied depending on the height of the trestle and the slope of the ground. All this layout was done by hand with no computers (Figure 5).

The actual logging was done by woodchoppers, with laborers or teamsters moving the wood to the flume either with horses or a tram and flume tenders keeping it moving down the flume.

Since almost all the trees could be made into firewood, McCune's operation became a huge clearcut (Figure 6). Trees were felled by hand using either a double-bitted axe or a one-man crosscut. The woodchopper would then use a one-man crosscut saw to cut the wood to four-foot lengths (Figure 7). The larger pieces were split for easier handling. Woodworkers were paid "by the cord" or by the day and frequently were paid only once a year. Wood was ricked or banked (stacked) where it was cut, awaiting the next operation which was to move the wood to the flume. This task was done by laborers.

In 1885, the woodchoppers went on strike. They had three main objectives: increase wages from $2.25 per day to $2.50; work as many hours as they wanted; and be able to purchase goods where they pleased.[7] There was no record found pertaining to the results of the strike.

Figure 6 – Area south of the Continental Divide and west of Highway 569 cut by McCune, ca. 1887. Sugarloaf Mountain is in the background. An estimated 55,000 cords of wood are stacked in the photograph. This amount of wood would not supply the fuel required to run the Anaconda smelter for a year. The photographer is standing by the flume, which meant all this wood had to be brought uphill by horses or a tram. Photograph courtesy of the Montana Historical Society photograph archives Pac 78-50.8. Photographer unknown.

Figure 7 – One-man crosscut saw used for cutting down and bucking up trees. 2006. The saw would only have a handle on one end. Found in Willow Creek. Photograph by B. John Losensky.

Figure 8 – Horse skidding logs to the flume, 1908. Horses played a major role in all methods used to get wood to the flume. Photograph courtesy of University of Montana Archives and Special Collections (77-173). Photographer unknown.

Several techniques were employed in moving the wood. For areas above the flume, the wood was placed on sleds in the winter, while wagons may have been used during the summer (Figures 8–9). These were pulled by horses to the flume. Sometimes a drag was used instead of a wagon. A drag consisted of two wheels, with one end of the wood supported by the wheels and the other end dragging on the ground. These methods worked well in the Mill Creek drainage, as the flumes were in the stream bottoms and almost all material could be moved downslope. For areas below the flume, sleds were less effective

Figure 9 – Remains of a skidding sled used to haul material to the flume. 1998. Found in the Allen sale. Photograph by B. John Losensky.

Figure 10 – Horses used to pack firewood. ca. 1900. PHOTOGRAPH COURTESY OF THE MILE HIGH NORDIC SKI EDUCATION FOUNDATION. PHOTOGRAPHER UNKNOWN.

and wagons may have played a more important role. Packhorses were also used to bring the wood upslope from difficult locations. A horse could pack between a quarter and a sixth of a cord for up to a half mile[8] (Figure 10).

Once the flume crossed the Continental Divide, it was located about mid slope, which meant that about half of the firewood was below the flume and had to be brought up to the flume. For short distances, this could be accomplished with the normal skidding methods mentioned previously. However, in areas where slope or distance made these methods impractical, a tram was constructed. This consisted of constructing a grade in a straight line down the slope (Figure 11). Iron rails were laid on cross ties on the grade. Rollers were placed at points where the terrain caused the cable to rub on the ties (Figure 12). A steam engine which powered a large cable spool was set up above the flume (Figure 13). Small tram cars were lowered on the cable to haul the wood to the flume. These cars were constructed on site and were about sixteen feet long and not quite three feet wide (Figures 14–15). A number of these would be hooked together to form a train (Figure 16).

Figure 11 – A tram used to bring material up to the flume. This tram was in Allen's sale and referred to in the text as the Little American Creek Tram, constructed ca. 1910. Similar trams were used in McCune's operation. Note the rollers installed in the center of the track to prevent the cable from damaging the ties. This tram was about one and a quarter mile long. PHOTOGRAPH COURTESY OF MONTANA HISTORICAL SOCIETY RESEARCH CENTER. PHOTOGRAPHER UNKNOWN.

Figure 12 – A handmade roller to support the tram cable where topography caused the cable to dig into the ground. They prevented the cable from breaking the ties of the tram. 1997. Note the wear in the center of the roller. See Figure 11, which shows the location of these rollers. PHOTOGRAPH BY B. JOHN LOSENSKY.

Figure 13 – Setting up a steam engine and winch for a tram, ca. 1908. Note the large spool that held the cable used to hoist the cars up the tram. The area has already been logged and piles of material can be seen on the right-hand side of the photograph. This may be the winch for the Bridge-Crooked John Tram. PHOTOGRAPH COURTESY OF MILE HIGH NORDIC SKI EDUCATION FOUNDATION. PHOTOGRAPHER UNKNOWN.

Figure 14 – Tram car with axles attached located adjacent to the Tenmile Creek Tram. 1998. Note the eye on the front of the tram car to attach cars together to make a train. PHOTOGRAPH BY B. JOHN LOSENSKY.

Figure 15 – Hook and chain that connected tram cars together to form a train. 1998. PHOTOGRAPH BY B. JOHN LOSENSKY.

Figure 16 – Train of tram cars at the top of Little American Creek Tram, ca. 1910. Camp Two is in the draw behind the man's right shoulder. PHOTOGRAPH COURTESY OF MILE HIGH NORDIC SKI EDUCATION FOUNDATION. PHOTOGRAPHER UNKNOWN.

Figure 17 – Loading dock adjacent to remains of the flume. 1998. The track for the tram siding for the Tenmile Tram was along the right side of the deck with remains of the flume on the left. PHOTOGRAPH BY B. JOHN LOSENSKY.

A siding from the tram was constructed adjacent to the flume so that the wood could be moved from the cars to the flume (Figure 17). When all the wood was removed from the site of a tram, it would be abandoned, with the power plant moved to the next site.

Wheels and axles were removed from the cars and new cars constructed at the new tram site (Figure 18). Cordwood was skidded to various points along the tram and stacked. The distance from the flume to the loading point was measured and a mark put on the cable so that the hoist operator knew when the cars were at the appropriate point for loading.

Figure 18 – Stack of abandoned tram cars with axles removed located near the end of the Sauna House Horse Tram on McCune's operation. 1998. Apparently, it was easier to construct new cars when the logging operation moved to a new area rather than moving the cars. PHOTOGRAPH BY B. JOHN LOSENSKY.

Additionally, a system of bells or whistles may have been used to communicate between the engineer and the loading crew. The cars were lowered by gravity to a stack of firewood, where they were loaded and then pulled up to the flume by the steam engine. The cars were run on a siding that paralleled the flume and unloaded directly into the flume. In operations where larger material was cut, it was decked above the flume and fed into the flume by the loading crew.

Figure 19 – A flume tender on Allen's Sale watching for log jams. Sugarloaf Mountain is in the background, ca. 1908. Photograph courtesy of Mile High Nordic Ski Education Foundation. Photographer unknown.

Two strings of cars may have been used so that one group was being loaded while the other was being unloaded into the flume. In some cases, a short flume was used to bring wood to the base of a tram. In other areas, where the ground was relatively flat, horse-drawn tram cars were used to bring the material to the base of the hoist tram. These cars would then be attached to the cable from the hoist and pulled up the hill. The horse-drawn trams followed the slope contour and were constructed with a favorable grade to the base of the hoist to reduce the effort required by the horse to pull the cars. Once loaded into the flume, the wood was floated down the flume guided by flume tenders (Figure 19).

Each flume tender was assigned about a two-mile stretch of flume that they were responsible for. He made sure the wood kept moving and did not cause a jam. He apparently also was responsible for making necessary repairs. Once the wood reached the end of the flume referred to as the "dump," a crew loaded the wood onto wagons, which took the wood three miles to the smelter (Figure 20). At some point after 1888, a railroad spur reached the "dump," and the wood was moved with railroad cars. The water from the flume left the end of the flume and eventually emptied into Mill Creek.

Payment to the wood choppers and haulers was made in October for the work done during the year at the Headquarters store in McCune's wood camp located in Section 18 T3N, R11W (Map 3). Workers at the dump were paid at the company store maintained by the Fluming Company in Anaconda. A number of these crews were subcontracted by the Fluming Company to do the work rather than work directly for the company.

Figure 20 – A view of the "dump" at the end of McCune's Flume reported to be over a half mile long, ca. 1887. Courtesy of the Montana Historical Society photograph archives Pac 78-50.2, photographer unknown.

By March of 1885, the papers reported between 200 and 300 men working for Caplice and McCune on Mill Creek.[9] (See Appendix C for a list of men employed by Caplice and McCune that year and their occupation.) By September, the *New Northwest* reported that 325 men were employed as wood choppers in Mill Creek area.[10] During 1885, the logging operation was confined to the Anaconda side of the Continental Divide. About 29,400 cords of wood were delivered to the company that year.[11] This amount represented less than 40 percent of what they were expected to deliver for the year. Based on what records are available, it seems that meeting the yearly contract amount was difficult.

John Caplice continued to be involved in retail sales in the state; an article in the *Weekly Anaconda Review* indicated he was doing business at New Chicago, Philipsburg, Missoula, Walkerville, and Butte.[12] However, by June 1885, he had closed his store in Missoula.[13] At the same time, the partnership between he and McCune continued to run a railroad construction operation. The *New Northwest* said that they had 100 teams and about 500 men working on the Helena branch on the Beaverhead River, where they were grading eight miles of rail bed.[14] They also had eighty men and sixty teams engaged in grading at the site of the new concentrator in Anaconda.[15]

Even at this early stage, impacts from the smelting operation were affecting Warm Springs Creek. The *New Northwest* stated that the poisonous matter from the smelter was entering the stream and that the company planned to cut a drain across the flats to the Deer Lodge River (present-day Clark Fork River) to get rid of the material.[16] Apparently, once the waste left the area and flushed down the river it was no longer considered a problem.

It became obvious to Caplice and McCune that there was not enough timber on the Anaconda side of the Continental Divide to meet their contract and that it would be necessary to extend the flume to the Big Hole side.[17] At least a portion of the area serviced by the flume in Mill Creek had been logged by Neagle during 1883–84. In addition, Henry Brundy, who had a sawmill in Mill Creek, logged an additional area to supply lumber for building projects in Anaconda and for the flume Spaker built.[18]

In 1885, the flume was extended across the Continental Divide; however, when they decided to extend the flume, the decision was made to log the area on the west side of the present highway. Consequently, the extension did not start from the end of the flume in Section 16 but rather in the northwest quarter of Section 4 T3N, R11W (Map 3). The new section crossed the divide on the west side of the present highway and about 50 feet downslope from the original flume.[19] This work was probably done by Jerry A. Gibson and completed in 1886[20] (Figure 21).

Sometime in 1886 or 1887, the flume was extended into Tenmile Creek. The flume up Sevenmile Creek (Ninemile Creek on early maps) may have been built at the same time. Probably in 1888, the main

Figure 21 – Crossing the Continental Divide, ca. 1887. The photograph is taken from the south side of the divide looking north. People on the picture are Alf, Fir, and Ray McCune standing near the horses; near the flume is Mat McCune, half-brother of Alfred W. McCune. In the background is George Davidson with the umbrella; next is Henry Geigerich with Alfred McCune sitting in front of him and Mr. C. Dudley. McCune's father is on the horse on the ridge and Mr. Kennedy is on the near horse. COURTESY OF THE MONTANA HISTORICAL SOCIETY PHOTOGRAPH ARCHIVES PAC 78-50.7. PHOTOGRAPHER UNKNOWN.

flume was extended to the Corral Creek area.[21] While information on logging activity given by various individuals was conflicting, the following dates probably represent a general timeline. Logging was active in Mill Creek in 1883–1885. By 1886, logging was occurring on both sides of the Continental Divide. Between 1887–1889, logging was active in Clear Creek west of the divide and in the Tenmile drainage east of the divide. During 1890 and 1891, logging continued in the McCune's Camp area, and by 1893 logging had reached Twelvemile Creek[22] (Maps 3–8).

Logging continued in 1886, but the amount recorded as received was only 3,502 cords.[23] The *Semi-Weekly Miner* reported that there were 80,000 cords cut near Mill Creek that would be flumed as soon as the new flume was completed.[24] By the end of the year the company had 13,000 cords at the end of the Williams Flume (which was in German Gulch), 75,000 cords at Mill Creek, and 20,000 cords west of Anaconda in other locations.[25] About 118,000 cords were cut by Caplice and McCune between 1884 and 1887, which was just over half of what their contract called for.[26]

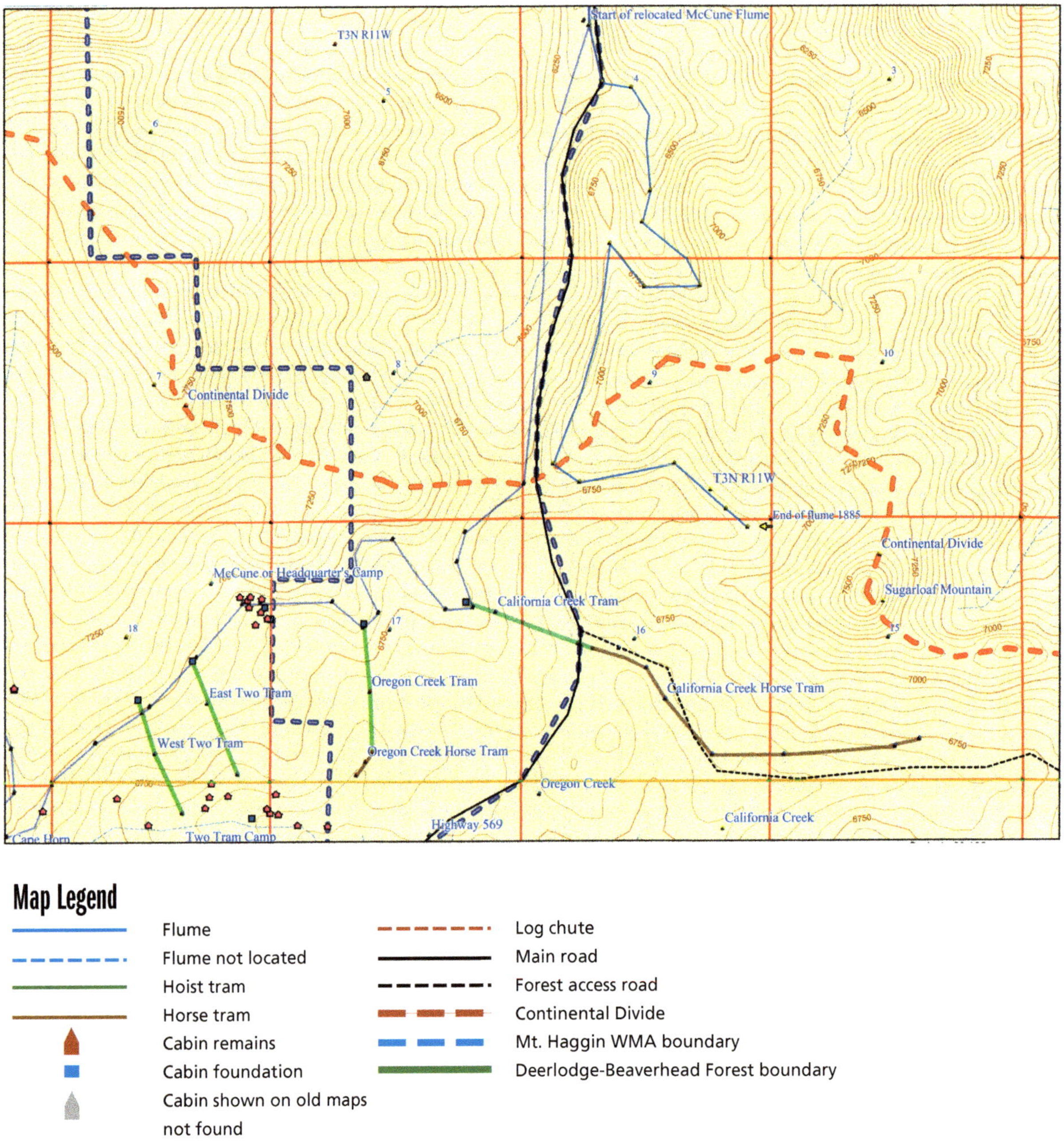

Map 3 – Map showing the relocated McCune Flume between the point of departure from the original flume to McCune Camp. It shows the location of McCune or Headquarters Camp and California and Oregon trams.

Other than failing to meet production goals, the operation appeared to be running smoothly, with no interference from any federal agencies. News about the flume operation was frequently published in the local papers and, with the number of people employed, there was no doubt that government officials knew that timber cutting was occurring on the public domain. Trespass cases were being brought against the Northern Pacific Railroad Company and the Montana Improvement Company for cutting 45,100,000 board feet of lumber from public domain.[27] Paying off the inspectors in a poker game must have been effective in preventing the closure of the flume.[28] While operations appeared to be moving well in the woods, developing political events would cause a major disruption in the partnership.

CHAPTER NINE

Caplice and McCune Work Camps

During the life of the logging operation, various settlements were established to support the loggers. Since most of the area in Clear Creek and Mill Creek is privately owned ground, investigation was not possible; however, old maps do show two camps: Camp Four and Wood Camp.[1] Little is known about these camps other than that Camp Four contained several tents. There was also a settlement near the "dump" for the workers loading the wagons and, later, the railroad cars. This settlement consisted of an office for the manager, a store, a blacksmith shop, a wheelwright shop, boarding houses, residence for the foreman, and other necessary buildings.[2] Another settlement was located around the Tenmile Saloon in the SE1/4 Section 28 T4N, R11W (Map 2) that may have housed a part of the logging crew working in that area.[3] The settlement consisted of a hotel, boarding house, store, and a few cabins.[4] Since flumes were constructed up Clear Creek for about three miles and Mill Creek for about four miles, it is highly likely that additional camps were in these drainages, although no information was found about them.

Several camps were surveyed east of and along the Continental Divide. Names were not found for some of these, so to aid in tracking them an arbitrary name was given to each by the author based on use or land features. This naming convention was also used to identify trams and flumes.

Sawmill Camp is located at the head of an unnamed branch of Mill Creek in Section 3 T3N, R11W (Map 4) on the Continental Divide. It was first established as a site for a sawmill during construction of the original flume and later used during the logging period. Remains of four cabins can be found along with a larger building that may have been used as a boarding house (Figure 22). Additional buildings such as a barn for the horses were probably here at one time as well.

A complex system of hoist and horse trams was used to log the area near this camp. The Sauna House Horse Tram, so named because remains of a sauna house were found nearby (Figure 23), was built to access the S ½ Section 3, the NE ¼ Section 10 and the NE ¼ Section 9 T3N, R11W (Map 4). It is about a mile long and was built on about a 2.5 percent favorable grade. Horses were used to pull the tram cars on these rail tracks from the logging area to the flume. The horse tram ended on a point above the flume and the firewood was dumped down a steep chute into a pond. At this point, the material was fed into the flume.

The East Sugarloaf Horse Tram was constructed to log the northeast slope of Sugarloaf Mountain. It is about 3,516 feet long on a 4 percent grade and ended in the middle of Section 10. From this point

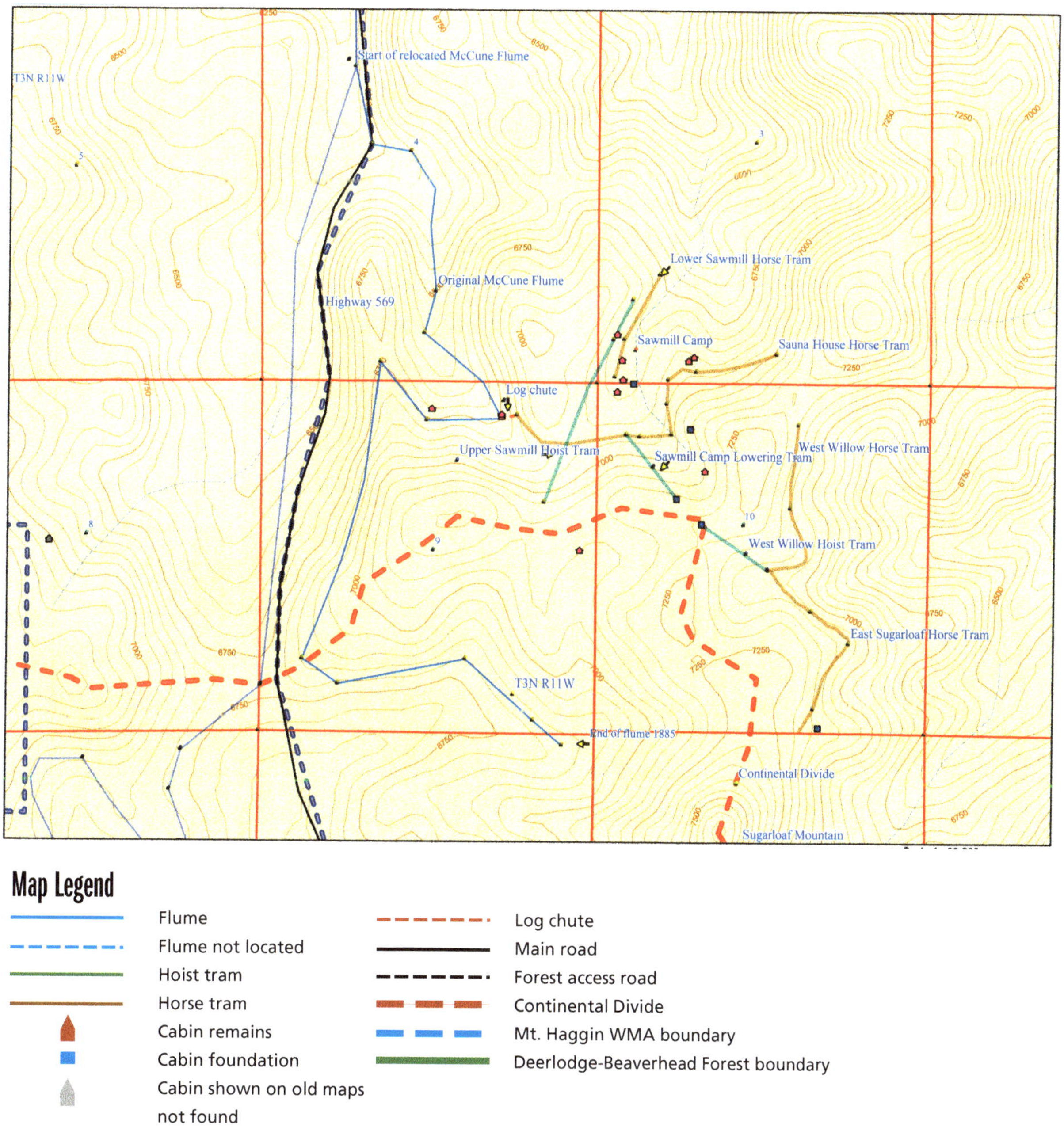

Map 4 – Map of Sawmill Camp Area showing complex of trams.

Figure 22 – Cabin located near Sawmill Camp. 1998. Note the heavy erosion on the slope behind the cabin. PHOTOGRAPH BY B. JOHN LOSENSKY.

the West Willow Horse Tram was built north to almost the section line between Sections 3 and 10 T3N, R11W so that the upper slope of West Willow Creek could be logged. The tram was about 3,667 feet long and built on about a 3.3 percent favorable grade.

These two horse trams met at the base of the West Willow Hoist Tram, which lifted the material to a ridge in the northwest quarter of Section 10. The West Willow Tram was about 1,649 feet long and gained about 122 feet in elevation. At this point, it was necessary to move the material downslope to the Sauna House Horse Tram.

On the ridge, a system of sidings was used to move the cars by gravity from the hoist tram to the Sawmill Camp Lowering Tram. From there the cars were lowered to the Sauna House Horse Tram (Map 4). The lowering

Figure 23 – Sauna house found near Sawmill Camp. 1998. It had no windows and a fire pit in the center. PHOTOGRAPH BY B. JOHN LOSENSKY

tram was about 1,642 feet long and dropped 280 feet. From there, the cars were pulled by horses to the site where the firewood was dumped into the small pond mentioned above. An additional two trams may have been located on the slope east of the camp, but heavy erosion has erased most of the evidence. This arrangement of trams required a good deal of handling of the wood by the loggers, which increased costs. It was the only site developed in this manner.

Once the operation crossed the Continental Divide, the base of operations was located at McCune or Headquarters Camp in the NE ¼ Section 18 T3N, R11W[5] (Map 5). At the time of investigation by the author there were remains of two barns, a blacksmith shop, a sawmill site, a store, a boarding house, and five cabins, one of which was the home of McCune (Figure 24). The sawmill was run by Mr. Joiner.[6] In addition, there were flattened areas that probably were the sites of other buildings, and the camp may have contained close to twenty cabins. An article in the *Butte Daily Miner* dated January 1, 1889, indicated there was an office for the manager, a store, blacksmith shop, wheelwright shop, boarding houses, residence for the foreman, and other buildings.[7] This camp became an important part of McCune's operation and was used until logging ceased. It even became a voting place during the 1888 congressional election and reported that forty-five votes had been cast.[8]

Figure 24 – Remains of the blacksmith shop in McCune. 1998. Note the slow recovery on this site because of logging and a fire in 1889. Photograph by B. John Losensky.

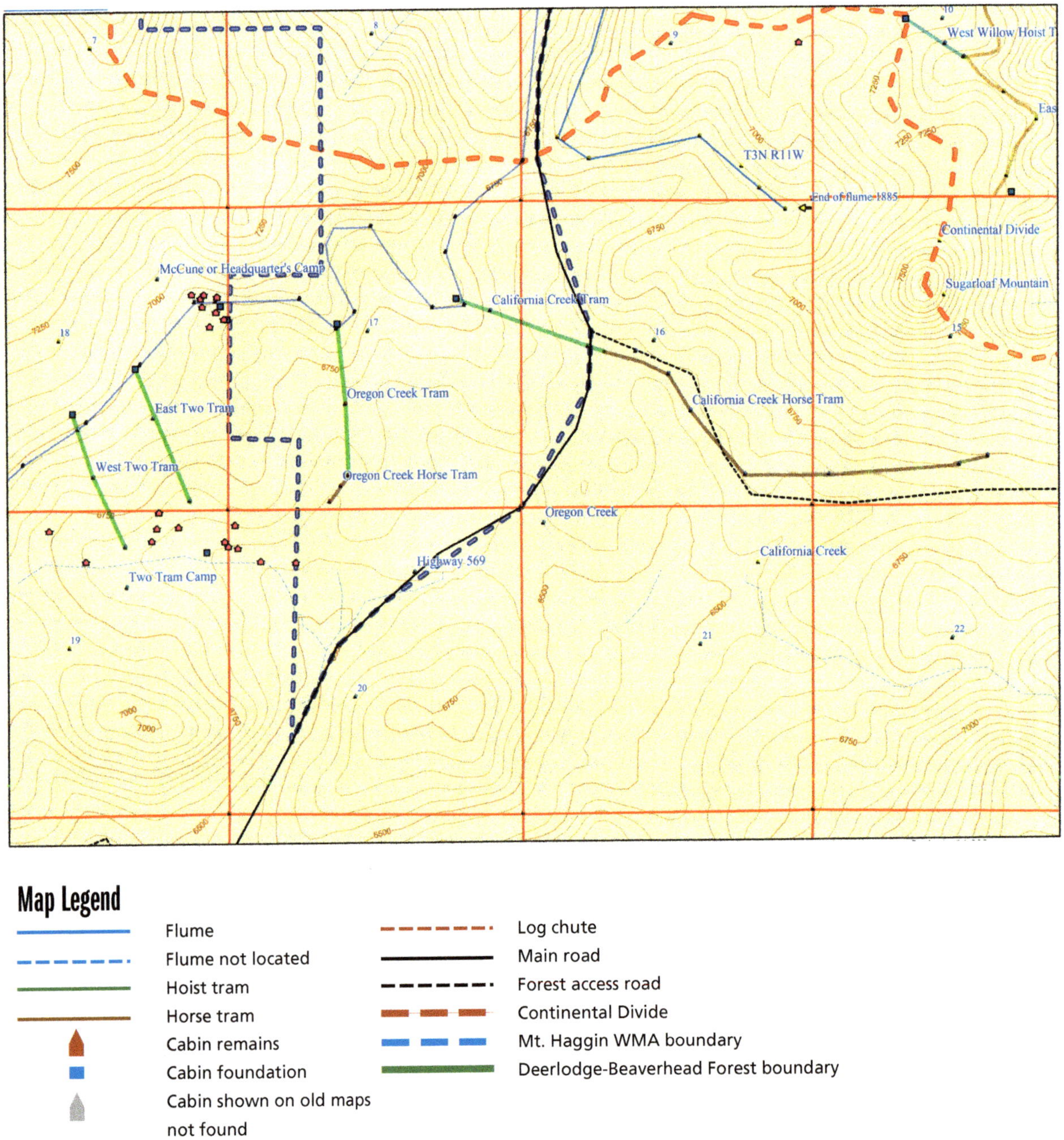

Map 5 – Map of McCune or Headquarters Camp Area and Two-Tram Camp Area.

In addition to the sawmill, two trams were supported by Headquarters Camp. The California Creek Tram provided access to California Creek and the south slope of Sugarloaf Mountain (Figure 25, Map 5).

The California Tram is about 2,900 feet long and gained about 226 feet to the flume. The California Creek Horse Tram that extended up California Creek ended at the base of this hoist. The horse tram was about one and a half miles long and built on a 2 percent favorable grade.

Figure 25 – Looking down the path of the California Tram. 1997. The meadow in California Creek can be seen in the top center of the photograph. Photograph by B. John Losensky.

The Oregon Creek Tram was located just east of Headquarters Camp and gave access to the southern portion of Section 17 T3N, R11W (Map 5). It was about 2,640 feet long and gained about 230 feet in elevation. There may have been a horse tram which moved wood to the end of this hoist, but severe erosion has destroyed most evidence.

In Section 19 T3N, R11W is located Two-Tram Camp, which supported the two trams located near the camp (Figure 26, Map 6). It contained at least one barn and eleven cabins. The East Two Tram is 2,520

Figure 26 – Cabin in Two-Tram Camp. 1997. This cabin is 12x12 feet with one door and no windows. It is roughly built and typical of most cabins used by the woodchoppers in the three sale areas. Photograph by B. John Losensky.

Figure 27 – A crew cabin 18x27 feet in size located in Sixmile Creek. 1997. It had a board floor and a roof made of slab wood. This represents a typical cabin found in a camp with a sawmill. PHOTOGRAPH BY B. JOHN LOSENSKY.

feet long and gained about 300 feet in elevation. The West Two Tram was similar in length and elevation gained. These trams provided access to a branch of Oregon Creek in Sections 18 and 19 T3N, R11W. The setup of these two trams so close together raises questions as to their purpose. The area is part of that shown in the photograph on page 28, Figure 6. The sheer volume of material needed to be moved to the flume may have made it necessary to place two trams here.

Past Two-Tram Camp is a very sharp turn in the flume on a steep slope into Sixmile Creek. It was referred to as Cape Horn and was the site of numerous breaks in the flume.[9]

There was a small camp at the head of Sixmile Creek (Keep Cool Creek on early maps) in Section 1 T3N, R12W that supported a sawmill during construction of the flume. The remains of the sawmill are there, along with two large cabins used for boarding (Figure 27). In addition, one barn was located along with three cabin sites (Map 6).

Figure 28 – Corkscrew curve in Sixmile area, ca. 1887. This section of the flume was referred to as the "corkscrew" and is in the Sixmile drainage. It demonstrates the complex engineering required to fit the flume to the landscape. Note the brush piles in the foreground that were piled after logging. COURTESY OF THE MONTANA HISTORICAL SOCIETY PHOTOGRAPH ARCHIVES PAC 78-50.6. PHOTOGRAPHER UNKNOWN.

Between Cape Horn and Sixmile Camp is an area on the flume referred to as the "Corkscrew." This curve represents a major feat with the tools available at the time (Figure 28).

The next camp was located at the head of Sevenmile Creek in the NW ¼ Section 2 T3N, R12W (Map 7). It consisted of one barn, two boarding houses, and five cabins (Figure 29).

Figure 29 – Sevenmile Camp. The picture shows three of the cabins located in Sevenmile Camp. 1997. PHOTOGRAPH BY B. JOHN LOSENSKY.

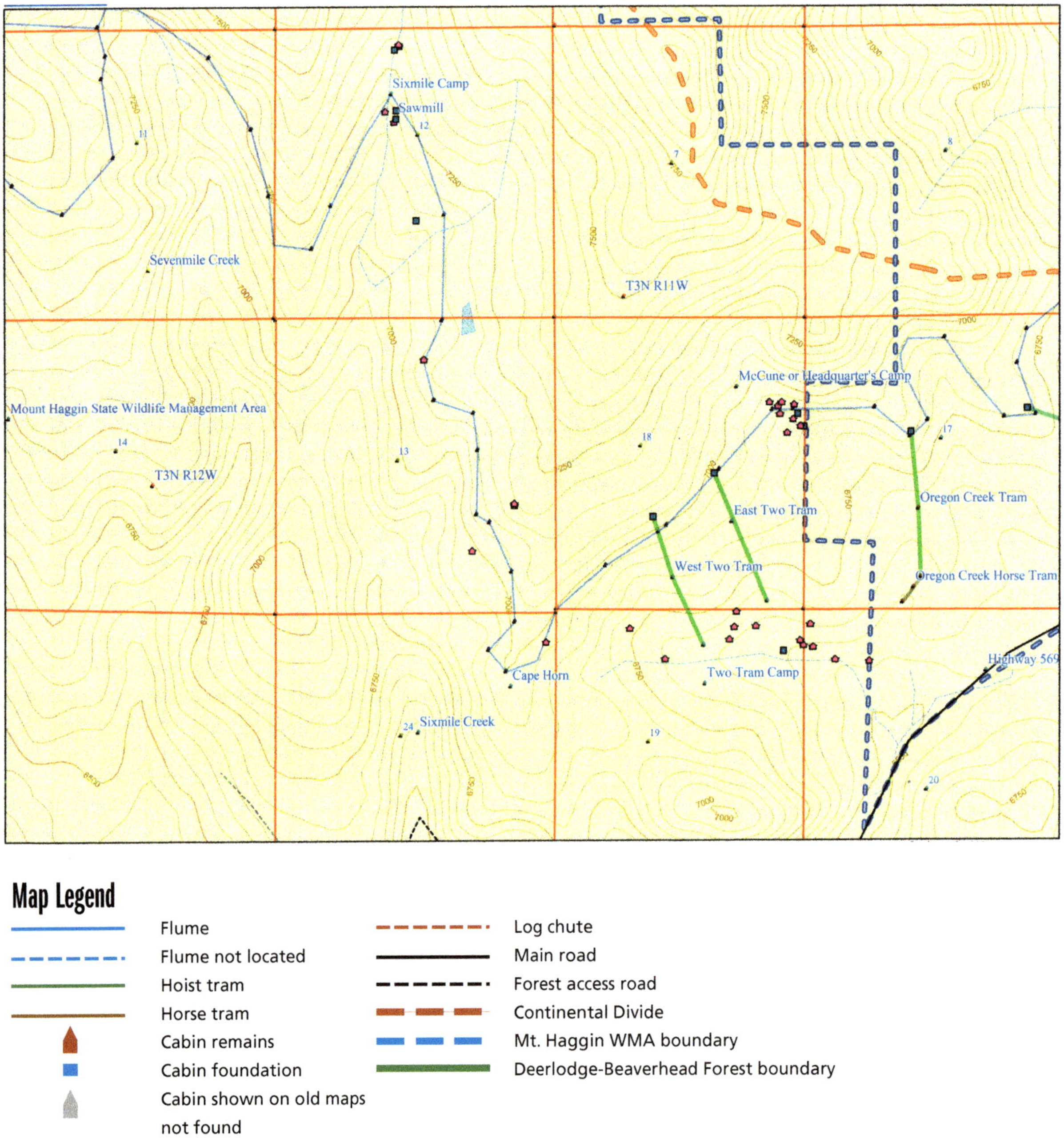

Map 6 – Map of Sixmile Camp Area.

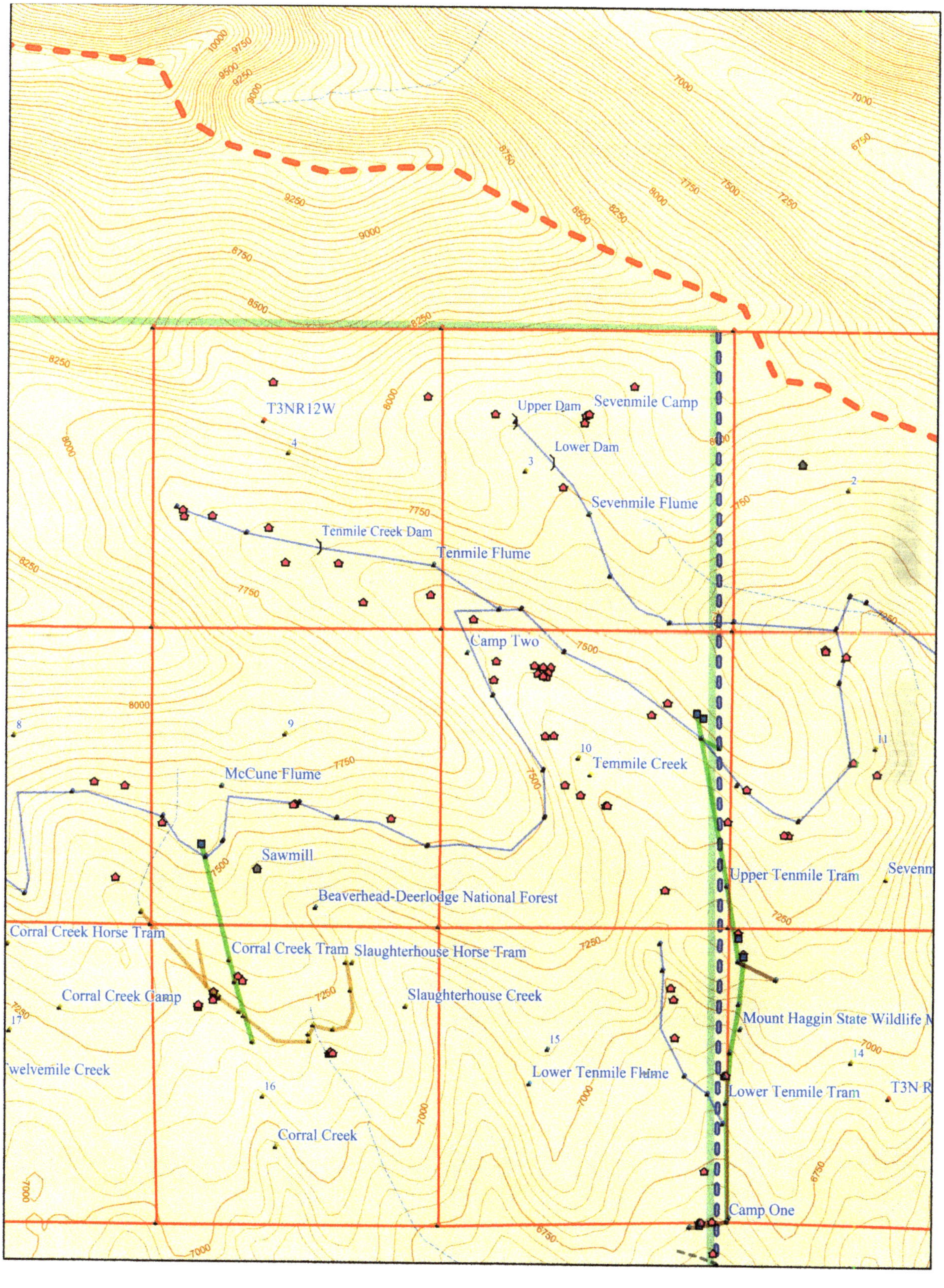

Map 7 – Map of Sevenmile and Tenmile Creek Area and Camps One and Two.

Figure 30 – Foundation in Camp One. It was 30x55 feet and located near the end of the tram. Its use is unclear and may represent a foundation for a sawmill or a large bunkhouse. 2001. PHOTOGRAPH BY B. JOHN LOSENSKY.

Figure 31 – Large horse barn in Camp Two on Tenmile Creek. 1999. It is 30x114 feet and divided into three rooms. This is one of the largest barns found on the sale. PHOTOGRAPH BY B. JOHN LOSENSKY.

Two other camps were located in Tenmile Creek.[10] Camp One was located at the bottom of the Tenmile Tram in the NE ¼ Section 22 T3N, R12W (Map 7). There may have been a sawmill here, as there is a large foundation in the camp (Figure 30). The remains of a barn and two cabins were also noted. There were additional flat spots and remains of a foundation also located in the camp.

Camp Two is in the NW ¼ Section 10 T3N, R12W (Map 7). There are two boarding cabins here, plus six cabins and one large barn 30 feet by 114 feet. The barn is divided into three sections by log walls (Figure 31).

The main flume originally ended in Tenmile Creek in the NWSW ¼ Section 4 T3N, R 11W. A large water storage dam was constructed about a half mile up the drainage above Camp Two which provided water for late season fluming (Figure 32). Water was also added at each stream crossing, as leakage was a problem. Camp Two provided support for this section of the flume and the Tenmile tram. After the upper Tenmile drainage was logged, the main flume was abandoned above the dam and the flume extended from near Camp Two another four and a half miles into Twelvemile Creek, where it ended (Map 8, Figure 33). The Tenmile Tram was built in stages and consisted of two trams built end to end. The first stage of the upper tram reached the NW ¼ Section 14 T3N, R12W. It was about 4,470 feet long and ended just before a steep drop in the terrain. A second hoist was set up here and another tram extended about 3,000

Figure 32 – Headgate in Tenmile Dam. View looking downstream at the headgate of the dam. 1997. This structure provided water for the fluming season. Photograph by B. John Losensky.

Figure 33 – Flume crossing Tenmile Creek, ca. 1887. Men on the wood piles are, left to right: H. Geigerich, Alf McCune, and C. Dudley. Behind the flume is a small group of trees with a woodchopper's cabin just to the left of them. Based on the height of the stumps, this area may have been logged in the wintertime. COURTESY OF THE MONTANA HISTORICAL SOCIETY PHOTOGRAPH ARCHIVES PAC 78-50.5. PHOTOGRAPHER UNKNOWN.

feet further down the slope. A system of siding moved the cars from the lower to the upper tram, probably with the aid of horses. A flume that extended up Tenmile Creek ended at the end of the lower tram. This flume was also of smaller size like that found in Sevenmile Creek. It was 3,525 feet long and had a gradient of about 7 percent.

After the wood was removed from this part of Tenmile Creek, the path of the lower tram was adjusted and extended down slope another 1,674 feet to Camp One. The total length of both trams was about one point seven miles and gained about 859 feet in elevation to the flume (Figures 34–36).

Figure 34 – Rock work to support the Tenmile Tram where it crosses the flume. 1998. Scattered pieces of wood can be seen in the flume path. PHOTOGRAPH BY B. JOHN LOSENSKY.

The last camp was in Corral Creek in the NW ¼ Section 16 T3N, R12W (Map 8). Remains found here consisted of two boarding cabins and six cabins (Figure 37). This camp supported the Corral Creek Tram, and at least one barn was probably located here. The tram was 3,640 feet long and gained 425 feet to the flume. The Corral

Figure 35 – Set of tram wheels found near the Tenmile Tram. 1998. Normally the wheels and axles were removed from the tram cars after its use was completed and the car bodies abandoned. The axles and wheels would have been used at the next tram site and attached to new cars constructed there. PHOTOGRAPH BY B. JOHN LOSENSKY.

Figure 36 – Cribbing on Tenmile Tram. This cribbing extended over a low spot to maintain the grade of the tram. 1997. PHOTOGRAPH BY B. JOHN LOSENSKY.

Creek Horse Tram accessed Corral Creek and was about one half-mile long on a favorable grade of 3 percent. Slaughterhouse Horse Tram provided access into Slaughterhouse Creek and was about 4,300 feet on a level grade. This tram may have continued to the northeast side of the drainage, but recent logging has destroyed much of the evidence on the ground. Both trams ended at the base of the Corral Creek Tram. There is other evidence that suggests additional horse trams were located here, but only short stretches could be found. A sawmill site was shown on a map in Slaughterhouse Creek in the area near the camp, but no remains were located.[11]

Figure 37 – Two-room cabin in Corral Creek Camp. This two-room cabin may have been used as the mess hall for the camp. 2001. It had two rooms with a log wall between the rooms. It is 22x55 feet and has three doors and six windows. PHOTOGRAPH BY B. JOHN LOSENSKY.

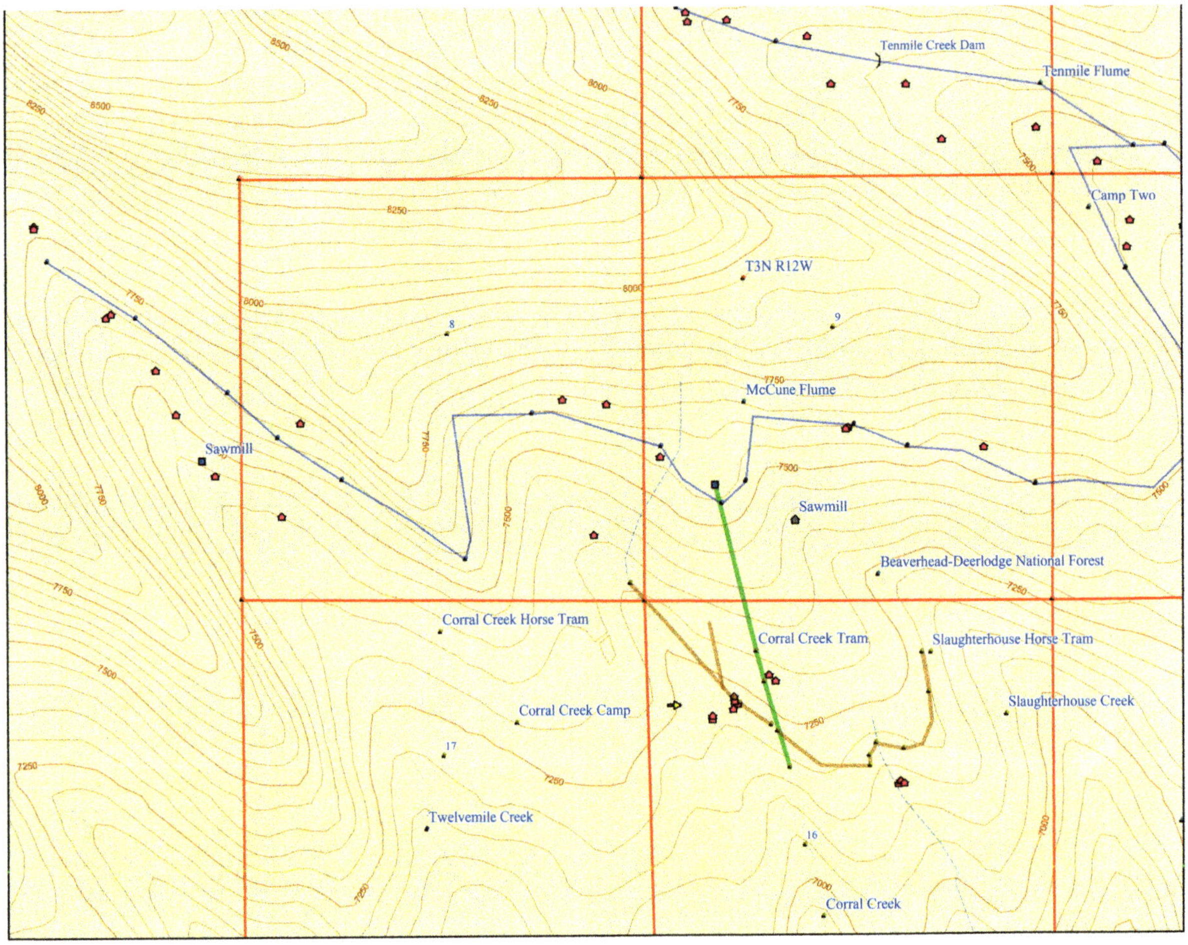

Map Legend

	Flume		Log chute
	Flume not located		Main road
	Hoist tram		Forest access road
	Horse tram		Continental Divide
	Cabin remains		Mt. Haggin WMA boundary
	Cabin foundation		Deerlodge-Beaverhead Forest boundary
	Cabin shown on old maps not found		

Map 8 – Map of Corral Creek Camp Area. The end of the flume is shown in Twelvemile Creek, plus the trams in Corral Creek.

CHAPTER TEN

Ousting Caplice

Operations of the fluming business seemed to go along smoothly for Caplice and McCune until politics became involved. To understand the breakup of the partnership, it is helpful to understand the politics of the time.[1] Deer Lodge County was formed in 1864 and Silver Bow County in 1881. Both were solidly Democratic. A Republican was wasting his time trying to run for office in either of these two counties. Between 1860 and the early 1900s, the Republicans controlled the White House except for Grover Cleveland's two terms, 1885–1889 and 1894–1898. The Republicans took little interest in controlling illegal cutting on the public domain and Marcus Daly took full advantage of this to fuel his operation. Unfortunately for Daly, during Cleveland's first term, he pushed for honesty in government, resulting in his Interior Secretary Lucius Lamar and Land Commissioner Andrew Jackson Sparks filing suits against companies that were illegally cutting on public lands.[2] One of those companies was the Montana Improvement Company (MIC) controlled by Andrew Hammond, Richard Eddy, and Edward Bonner.[3] This company was the main source of timber that Daly needed for his mines. If Cleveland was reelected in 1888, Daly was going to lose his source of cheap lumber and fuel, as several trespassing cases against the Montana Improvement Company were to come to the courts that year. At the same time, there was trouble in the Democratic Party, particularly in the east over tariff laws, and there were signs that the Republican Party would probably win the next election, resulting in an uncertain outlook for Daly's wood supply. If the Republicans won the election and Montana had a Democratic congressman, he would have difficulty being recognized by the Republican administration and could do little to control the case against the Montana Improvement Company. If, on the other hand, Montana had a Republican congressman, he could use his party's affiliation to control the government's actions in the timber case. Daly felt the only way out of the dilemma was to elect a Republican, which meant getting Silver Bow and Deer Lodge counties to vote Republican that year. William Clark, Daly's nemesis, was running as the Democratic candidate and Thomas H. Carter from Helena as the Republican candidate. While Clark was recognized throughout the state and considered a shoo-in, Carter was basically an unknown and described as spindly and rather awkward looking. Clark being the candidate was a major concern for Daly. Since Clark obtained most of his timber from railroad lands, he would not be affected by a crackdown on cutting on public lands. Also, there was no love lost between the two and Clark would probably use any means available to cause Daly trouble. If Clark was elected, it was almost certain that he would spend little time worrying about Daly's trespass cases and may even help them along behind the scenes. Consequently, Daly, along with Hammond and Bonner, began a campaign to get Carter elected. Since Daly was recognized as a Democrat, he had to work somewhat secretly. A major portion of the population in Butte and Anaconda either worked for Daly or were indirectly tied to him, as was the case with the Caplice and McCune partnership. Daly quietly met with his foremen and others and explained to them how he expected their crews to vote if they wanted to stay employed. Since the secret ballot had not yet been adopted, it was a simple matter for the foremen to check the ballots from his crew and make necessary corrections as needed to assure that a "proper" ballot was cast. Daly continued to round up votes without Clark's knowledge and was able to keep his activity quiet. It is not surprising that Daly could get his crews to go along and keep quiet about the plan. Many of his workers were newly arrived from Europe and needed a job to survive. Being blackballed by Daly was a sure way of losing all hope of a job in the Butte-Anaconda area. Eventually, Daly approached John Caplice about getting his woodchoppers to vote for Carter. Surprisingly, Caplice would not go along with Daly's plan and told Daly his workers could vote as they chose and he would not pressure them. This aggravated Daly, not only because the Caplice and McCune crews represented around 300 votes, but also because he was used to getting his way. In the hopes of pulling off his ploy, Daly went to McCune and told him he wanted Caplice out of the partnership, and he would provide the money to buy him out. It is unclear if McCune agreed to pressure his crew, but it is apparent that if he did not then Daly would have cancelled his wood contract.[4] On March 5, 1887, the *Semi-Weekly Miner* reported that a court case was listed on the docket for A.W. McCune vs. John Caplice.[5] The case may have been settled without going to trial, as the *Semi-Weekly Miner* on April 6, 1887, reported that "*Messrs. Caplice and McCune have dissolved their partnership. . . . Mr. Caplis* [sic] *retiring with a handsome profit on his original investment.*"[6] James B. Haggin, representing the Anaconda Gold and Silver Mining Company, released John Caplice from the obligation of the contract in April 1887, but McCune continued to be liable. With the dissolution of the partnership, a new company was formed on May 27, 1887, called the Anaconda Fluming Company. The original members were Alfred McCune, Henry Geigerich, William Hoge, William M. Thornton, and Arthur L. Kempland.[7] McCune owned 46 percent of the stock. Daly and officers of the Fluming Company owned the rest, and Daly effectively controlled the new company. Eventually, this would lead to problems for McCune.

When the dust settled, Carter was elected, to the amazement of loyal Democrats. Clark realized that Daly had ruined his chances to go to Congress, and the war of the Copper Kings began in earnest.

CHAPTER ELEVEN

The Last Gasp—1887–1896

After the departure of John Caplice, the business of getting wood to the mill became the focus of the Anaconda Fluming Company. A notice in the *Semi-Weekly Miner* in 1887 stated that fluming would begin about the 15th of May, and they expected to flume about 60,000 cords.[1] Currently, the smelter was using 125 cords of wood and 180 tons of coal every day.[2] In addition, 112 cords were being shipped to the mines in Butte every day.[3] The flume had been extended over the Continental Divide and was about twenty-two miles long.[4] This would indicate the flume had reached Headquarters Camp (McCune) near the present-day Mule Ranch. While the contract called for delivering 75,000 cords a year, only 60,000 cords were planned for 1887. This goal was missed, with a little under 50,000 cords flumed that year. An ad in the *Butte Daily Post* offered work for 300 woodchoppers as efforts were made to increase production to meet the demands of the company.[5] While this contract represented a major source of wood for the company, it only covered a portion of their needs as production at the smelter and mines increased. For example, a contract was given to the Kleinschmidt Company in 1887 to supply 10,000 cords for $4.75 a cord. Ten carloads were to go to the Anaconda mine and fifteen carloads to the smelter every day.[6] It was reported in the following year that forty-five cars a day were coming into Butte carrying twelve cords per car besides what was going to Anaconda.[7] With this increased demand, a request for bid was published in the *Butte Miner* to extend the flume five miles from Tenmile Creek to Twelvemile Creek in order to expand the logging area and meet the company's needs.[8]

Meanwhile, Daly became concerned about the rate the railroad was charging the company to haul ore from Butte to Anaconda. Efforts were made to negotiate lower rates without success. Finally, in January 1889, it was announced that the Anaconda Company would build their own railroad to haul ore from the mines, to be known as the Butte, Anaconda & Pacific Railroad (BA&P).[9] However, it was not until February of 1893 that the grading was completed. A flume was constructed in German Gulch to float the ties being cut there to the railroad grade, and between 600 to 700 men worked to build the railroad. It was expected that the rails would reach Anaconda by the end of September 1893.[10] In December of that year, the Montana Union Railroad derailed an engine near the ore dumps and served injunctions to prevent BA&P from clearing the wreck so that the last few feet of rail could not be laid.[11] This delaying tactic worked for a while, but finally, on January 1, 1894, the first ore train arrived on the BA&P railroad from Butte.[12]

In April 1889, the flume was again started, and the Fluming Company expected to bring down 200 cords of wood per day. It was estimated that 45,000 cords were already banked and ready to be brought down.[13] Fires played an important role in the logging operations that year, spawning numerous articles in the local newpapers.[14] In August 1889, a fire burned six miles of the flume in Clear Creek and one mile in Mill Creek, along with about 500 cords of wood. A few days later, a fire had started near the Anaconda Fluming Company camp, where 75,000 cords of wood were banked.[15] Over 100 men were sent out to the camp to fight the fire and additional men were requested.

Trouble was brewing between McCune and Daly. With the formation of the Anaconda Fluming Company, McCune lost control of his company, since Daly owned or controlled over 50 percent of the company shares. Daly did not need to make a profit from the fluming operation because the cheaper he could make that operation, the more money he made from his copper operation. McCune, on the other hand, was dependent on the business to make money. Henry Geigerich oversaw the business for McCune and held some shares in the fluming company. Years later, when a suit was brought against the Anaconda Company, he stated in his deposition that matters became so unpleasant that he quit the company and moved to Canada. He stated that the Anaconda Copper Company did not live up to the contract with the fluming company and that late payments put the fluming company in constant financial difficulties.[16] Logging, however, continued at a high rate, and by the fall of 1891, 180,000 cords were at the mouth of the flume and another 250,000 cords were piled along the flumes near Anaconda. It was said that the season's cut was the largest ever known in the county.[17] Between 1888 and 1891, 266,600 cords of wood were cut and delivered to the company by McCune's operation.[18]

In the spring of 1892, there were again articles in the local papers about the logging and the Mill Creek Flume. An estimated fifteen carloads of wood were being hauled from the end of the flume to the smelters every day. This represented about 180 cords a day.[19] Again more help was needed, and a notice seeking twenty-five teamsters and laborers to bank cordwood for the fluming company was published.[20] An article later in the year in the *Anaconda Standard* commented on how the smelting industry was dependent on the fluming and wood business. It stated that the smelters in Anaconda used 500 cords per day, or about 15,000 cords a month. Of this amount, 300 cords came from Mill Creek and 200 cords from a fluming operation near Elliston, Montana. The two suppliers employed about 475 men in their operations. The operations represented a sizable investment, as the flumes had to be constructed and were expensive to maintain. The woodcutters were said to be well paid, receiving between $2.50 to $3.00 per day.[21] Even with all this activity and reports in the local papers, there was no indication that the federal government made any attempt to control the cutting. While the woodcutters made a reasonable wage, the Anaconda Fluming Company was marginally getting by. Daly reduced the price the fluming company received from $3.49 to $3.33 per cord, and that reduction, along with slow payments by the company, made it difficult for the fluming company to make a profit. Henry Geigerich stated that the cost of tree falling (from $1.10 to $2 per cord), hauling costs (from 50 cents to $1.25), and the costs of fluming the material to the "dump" left little room for profit. He stated that the fluming company was issued a license in 1893 to run a saloon for $45 and another to sell merchandise for $10 to supply groceries and other items to the workers. He claimed that this income provided a small profit for the company.[22]

In the spring of 1895, operations were starting up for another year of fluming in Mill Creek. It was reported that repairs were being made to the flume. The snow, however, was still three to four feet deep, and hauling with wagon or sled was difficult because the warm days made the snow soft.[23] The flume at that time had reached Twelvemile Creek and was about twenty-five miles long. While there was plenty of wood available in this drainage, the length of the flume and expense to maintain it, along with the reduced payment for the wood, made the operation marginal. In addition, the availability of suitable coal was slowly replacing the reliance on wood for fuel. An article in the *Semi-Weekly Miner* in 1884 predicted: *"The question of fuel supply for future demands is only second in importance to that of our mineral development and the recent opening up of valuable coal veins in the various parts of the Territory, gives ample assurance that in the not distant future, coal will in great measure, supplant wood as the fuel for the supply of our mills, furnaces and manufactures."*[24] The Northern Pacific Railroad already had a mine they were actively working near Bozeman, and this area was also being developed by other private individuals.[25] Consequently, as the infrastructure of the railroad across Montana developed, coal from various mines in the state and Wyoming were tested for suitability for the smelting process. The *Weekly Anaconda Review* on December 2, 1886, stated that the first shipment of ten cars of coal arrived from Rock Springs, Wyoming. At that time, the Anaconda Smelting Company was using 180 tons of coal and 125 cords of wood daily.[26] It was also noted that the mine and mill were closed most of February that year because of the lack of coal, as the railroad had been closed by a snow slide.[27] The mill was closed again in 1889 because of another lack of coal. By then they were using 400 tons per day.[28] Based on an article on December 19, 1888, in the *Semi-Weekly Miner*, coal at this time was also being used by the public for heating purposes. The article stated: *"Colonel Lloyd pronounces it is a good quality of lignite (Sand Coulee coal) and has some on trial now. It has been used at the Parrot & Butte Reduction Works but is not satisfactory as a smelting coal. For heating purposes, however, it has been found to be all that is required."*[29] Coal use continued to increase, and in 1890, the Anaconda Company used 18,327 tons of coal in the month of May.[30] By 1895, coal represented a major fuel. Between January 1, 1894, and November 30, 1894, the mines used 221,084 tons of coal and 68,608 cords of wood. The coal was from Rock Springs, Wyoming, and Sand Coulee and Belt, Montana. Of the wood, 30,157 cords came from Elliston, Montana, and 38,597 cords came from the Bitterroot Valley. Additional wood came from the area surrounding Butte and Anaconda.[31] The coal from Rock Spring was found to be suitable for smelting and, by November 1895, changes were made to the grates so that coal could be used exclusively for fuel and wood was no longer used.[32]

Changing to coal had a major impact on the demand for fuel wood. Since McCune was cutting just firewood for the Anaconda Company, this change basically eliminated a major portion of his market. At the same time, problems between McCune and the Anaconda Company over payment for wood received came to a head. Prior to the breakup of Caplice and McCune, the partnership had some control in their negotiations with the company. However, with Caplice's departure and the formation of a new company, McCune now was a minority owner in his own business. It was not necessary for the Anaconda Company to make a profit from their Anaconda Fluming Company, as a cheaper cost of fuel would translate into more profit from their copper. Consequently, once the volume for the original contract was met, Daly made several reductions in the price paid for the cordwood, which adversely affected McCune's business. In addition, there was a period when the payments made to the Fluming Company were less than the contract price, resulting in a lot of confusion as to what was owed to the Fluming Company. A series of letters were exchanged between 1894 and 1896 to sort out this problem. The Fluming Company sent letters to the smelting section and the mines section of the Anaconda Company stating that they were owed sixteen cents more per cord for wood delivered between November 1894 and July 31, 1895. This action resulted in the smelting section sending a letter dated October 19, 1895, to the mines section to determine if the mines section had received a similar letter. They also wanted to know if Mr. Daly had been consulted. A written response on the bottom of the letter stated: *"Yes, I have spoken to Mr. Daly, and he says to pay no attention to the claim. If they are willing to accept what I have to their credit in settlement, I will pay, otherwise, I will not."*[33] However, a statement showing wood received by the company between June 1895 and April 1896 had the following handwritten footnote: "*On August 3, 1896, having been advised by our lawyers that the Fluming Company would beat us in the suit they were going to bring against us to recover 16 cts. Per cord more on all wood delivered to the mines and works, we issued check to the Fluming Company for $98,739.31.*"[34] This amount represents over three and a half million dollars in 2022 dollars.

Finally, in October of 1895, a report in the *Anaconda Recorder* stated that the Mill Creek Flume had been closed permanently. The reason given was the length of the flume and the expense to operate.[35] Thus, with this brief statement, one of the largest fluming operations to have occurred in Montana ended. Over 700,000 cords were cut and flumed to Anaconda and Butte. McCune closed his operations in Montana and moved to Salt Lake City, where he was involved with a trolley car company and various mining ventures in Peru. While there is no doubt that the availability of coal and the high maintenance cost for the flume were major issues in closing the operation, other factors also played a part in the closure. The relationship between Daly and McCune was at an all-time low, and having to pay McCune the additional sixteen cents per cord would have resulted in Daly canceling the contract under the best of conditions. There was also a renewed effort on the part of the government to stop the taking of wood from the public domain, and a few small operations, including some prominent people in the area, were taken to court.[36] While there was no apparent attempt to investigate the Mill Creek Flume, it was only a matter of time before that would occur.

CHAPTER TWELVE

Other Operations

The closure of McCune's flume, however, did not mark the end of the use of flumes for transporting wood to the Butte-Anaconda area. As Daly's copper production increased, he needed additional sources of wood to power his mining operations until coal was more readily available. One of the first of these was near Elliston, Montana, on Little Blackfoot Creek. Daly started the Elliston Fluming Company in 1889, and eventually nine miles of main flume and seven miles of feeders were developed to remove and move the wood. A loading point was located about a half mile east of town by the Northern Pacific Railroad. During its operation, an average of twenty-five cars a day carried the wood to Anaconda. This operation continued until 1894, or about the time the smelters were converted to coal. During its peak in 1891, they had a payroll of $80,000 a month and 600 men cutting wood or working on the flume. Over 250,000 cords were removed during the life of the company and used to fire the smelters.[1]

In 1894, when cutting was beginning to wind down on McCune's operation, a new company began cutting in the adjacent Willow Creek drainage. While McCunes's operation was strictly cutting firewood, other operations, while cutting some firewood, focused on material for the mines. Richard E. DeKay and his father Augustus A. DeKay, along with Walter C. Staten, formed the Willow Creek Fluming Company, organized to cut wood, lumber, and ties for twenty years between 1895 and 1915. A notice placed in the *Anaconda Standard* on December 15, 1894, listed the area to be cut in Willow Creek and an estimated volume of 85,000 cords.[2] Augustus was from Canada and Richard DeKay was born in Minnesota in March 1870; little else is known about the Dekays. No other mention of Walter Staten can be found, and he may have left the company. Special Agent A.W. Lafferty of the General Land Office (GLO) sent a letter dated July 6, 1906, to the Commissioner of the GLO in which he stated that R.E. DeKay and his father constructed the flume in Willow Creek.[3] It was about five and a half miles long and ran from the Willow Creek Station on the Butte, Anaconda & Pacific Railroad (BA&P) to the SW ¼ Section 7 T3N, R10W near where the sawmill site is located (Map 9).

The company was plagued by suits over construction and management. In 1896, Annie DuBey sued for $3,000 in damages against the Willow Creek Fluming Company for constructing a flume across her land in the NW ¼ Section 29 T4N, R10W. The suit claimed that the company began construction of the flume without permission of the landowner. An injunction was issued to prevent further construction.[4] This action started a long string of court cases between the two parties. The injunction was dissolved by the court sometime around March 6, 1896.[5] In April of 1898, R.E. DeKay, owner of the Willow Creek Flume, brought charges against DuBey for malicious mischief in breaking down a gate on his property.

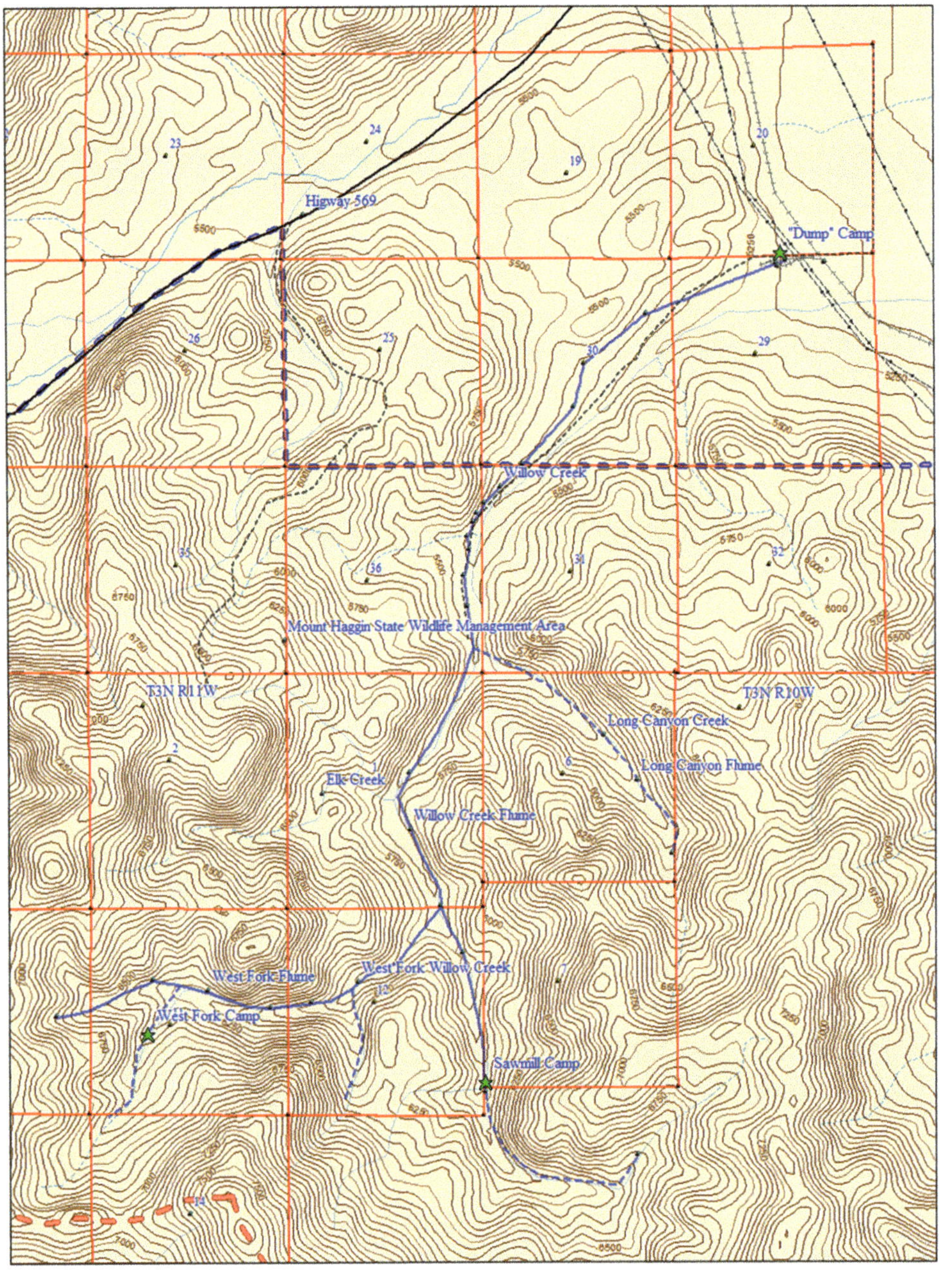

Map Legend

- Flume
- Flume not located
- Hoist tram
- Horse tram
- Cabin remains
- Cabin foundation
- Cabin shown on old maps not found
- Log chute
- Main road
- Forest access road
- Continental Divide
- Mt. Haggin WMA boundary
- Deerlodge-Beaverhead Forest boundary

Map 9 – Map of Willow Creek flumes.

This case was apparently dropped.[6] Later that year, the ranch of Annie and Charles DuBey was sold at sheriff's sale to satisfy a judgment in the case of John Lewissohn against them.[7]

In January 1900, R.E. DeKay filed suit to collect $20 that Charles DuBey owed him.[8] In June of 1900, Charles DuBey sued Peter Trundell and Augustus DeKay for $300 that he alleged was owed him for 200 cords of wood.[9] The original damage suit filed in 1896 continued in the courts, and in November of 1901, the case was tried and the jury taken to the field to review the damage that had occurred. The result of that visit fixed the amount of damage as $100 ($3,280 in 2022 dollars) for allowing the flume to overflow.[10]

Augustus was committed to the Montana State Hospital in Warm Springs in July of 1901 because of mental issues and subsequently died before November of that year. At that time, Richard was named executor of the estate and he and his sister Flora (DeKay) Meinhart were listed as sole heirs.[11] The will of Augustus gave 75 percent of the company to Richard and 25 percent to Flora. Flora and Richard did not get along and, in December of 1901, she sued her brother for his handling of the company. She felt he had misapplied and took large amounts of money belonging to her. At that time, the company had 3,600 cords of wood cut and $2,000 in cash, plus the value of the flume, which was estimated at $16,000 (about $561,000 in 2022 dollars).[12] She claimed that Richard refused to make an accounting or let her see the books. She also claimed that since the previous April, 1,500 cords of wood were sold for $4,200 and all she got was $140. She requested a full accounting and wanted the partnership dissolved.[13] The case was settled in March of 1902, when the judge ruled that there was no evidence of property being lost, so the circumstances did not warrant appointment of a receiver.[14]

After the case was settled, the company was put up for sale and Nels Pearson bought the operation, probably in the latter part of 1902.[15] Richard moved his family to Yakima, Washington, where in 1910 he was the proprietor of an ice plant.[16] No other information was found on Flora. During the time of operation, DeKay removed about 4,000 cords a year, or over 32,000 cords over the eight years.[17]

Nels Pearson was born is Skane, Sweden, on November 3, 1867, and came to America at the age of thirteen, first to Leadville, Colorado, and then, in 1886, to Butte.[18] He got a job pushing a wheelbarrow in the Parrot Mine for a while and then went to Havre, Montana, where he became involved in a coal mine. He then decided to homestead some land near Whitefish, Montana. In 1891, he sold the homestead for $3,000 and thirteen horses and headed back to Anaconda. He decided to go into the logging business in the Gregson area (near present-day Fairmont Hot Springs). In 1896, he was in the Flathead Valley running a crew cutting railroad ties. Upon completion of the contract, he came back to Anaconda and bought out the DeKay interest to the Willow Creek Fluming Company and began cutting stulls and props for the Butte mines.

When Pearson took over the operation, cutting had occurred for the previous eight years, and the main flume was already in place. It is not known when the branches up the side drainages were constructed, but they were probably added during DeKay's operation.

The first branch went up Long Canyon and was about 1.5 miles long. The branch up the West Fork Willow Creek was about 2.2 miles long and another branch that extended up an unnamed fork of the West Fork was about 0.85 miles[19] (Map 11). Because of the location of the flume in the stream bottoms, hoists and horse trams were not needed to move the wood, as all the material could be moved by horses downhill.

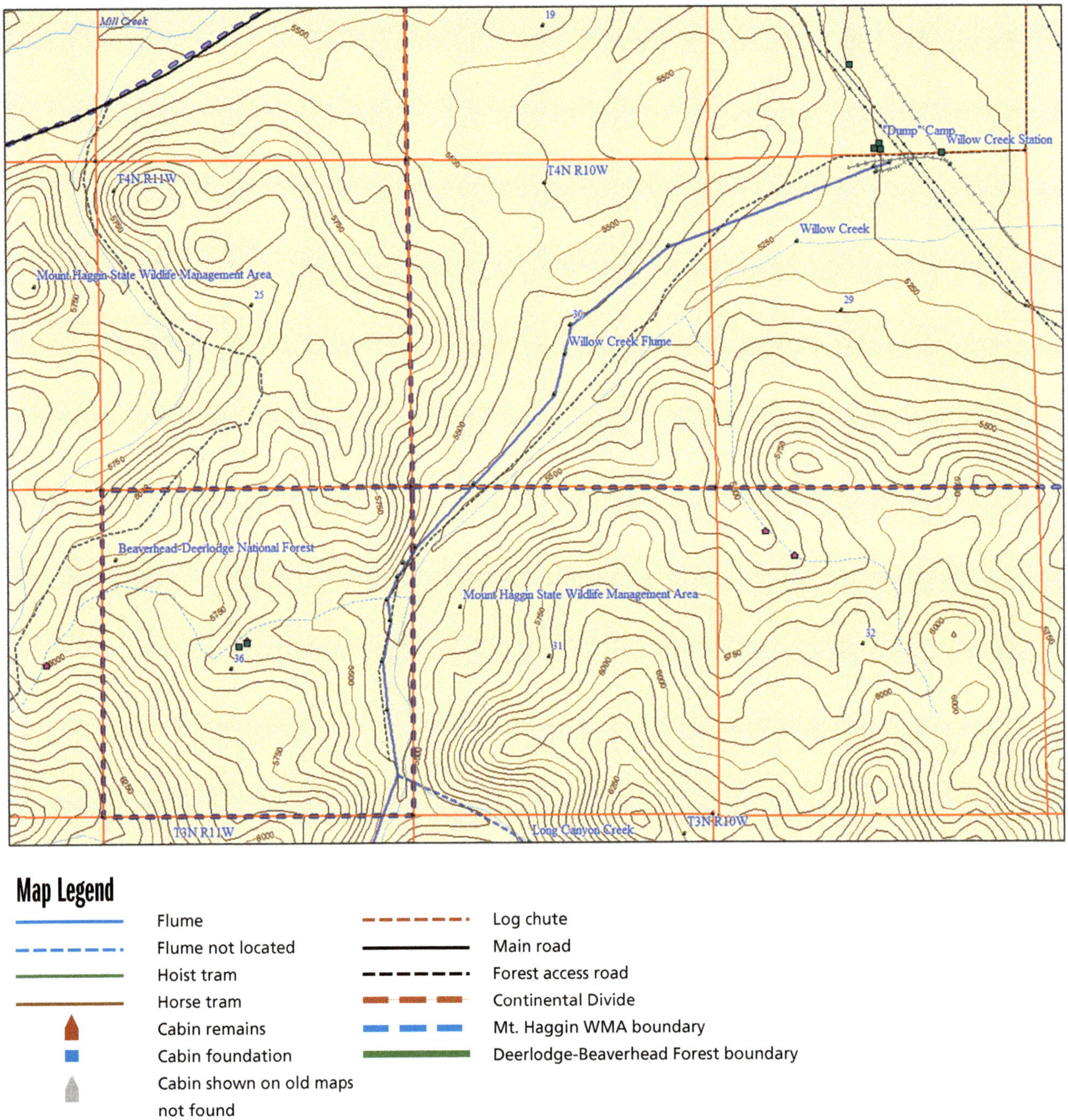

Map 10 – Map of lower Willow Creek showing the "dump" area by the railroad.

The Willow Creek Flume had access to the BA&P Railroad and a siding was situated where the present Willow Creek Road crosses the railroad (Map 10). Old railroad maps located at the Butte Historical Society show a spur labeled the "Willow Creek Wood Spur" starting about 300 feet south of the Willow Creek Road and then turning west and running parallel to the road.[20] It splits into two branches, with the branch adjacent to the road 1,120 feet long and the other 754 feet. Both spurs were taken up in 1918, but evidence of the grades can still be seen on the ground.

The "dump" camp was situated about 760 feet west of the crossing of the railroad on the north side of the road. This site was used by the crew that moved the wood from the flume to the rail cars. It consisted of a barn, house, and bunkhouse. Evidence of the camp is almost gone; only a partial outline of some of the buildings still remain. The remains of a well and some debris are also present. Willow Creek Station consisted of a building six feet by eight feet with a platform 132 feet by 8 feet. No remains are left of the station. It was located on the east side of the tracks, just north of where the county road crosses the railroad. To the west, near the end of one of the spurs, are the remains of a stone building. This may also have also been part of the siding operation.[21]

Between 1902 and 1906, Nels Pearson employed between eighteen and thirty men in the operation. While the flume at Elliston and the Willow Creek operation under Dekay management only cut cordwood, Pearson was producing stulls, lagging, converter poles, and cordwood that he sold in the local market.[22] Pearson continued logging in Willow Creek until 1910, when he was hired by the Mines Timber

Figure 38 – Remains of the flume in West Fork Willow Creek. 2004. Photograph by B. John Losensky.

Company to oversee the Allen operation covered in Chapter 13. When he left the Willow Creek Fluming Company, he put his two sons-in-law in charge of the Willow Creek operation.[23]

Brothers Isaac and Charles Johnson continued logging until about 1916, when operations ceased in this drainage. Meanwhile, they had started logging west of Georgetown Lake by 1912. Overall, Pearson was involved in logging in the Anaconda area until about 1926. Evidence for the Willow Creek Flume is difficult to find because of its location adjacent to Willow Creek or one of its tributaries (Figure 38). Yearly spring runoff resulted in much of the structure being washed away or buried. In contrast, most of McCune's flumes traversed the side slope and were not subjected to water erosion. In addition, no evidence was found that horse or hoist trams were used, as the logs could be moved downslope by horses in just about all cases. Only one sawmill set was located at the head of the Willow Creek Flume. Remains of the boiler mark the spot along with other items (Figures 39–40). Material for the flumes apparently was hauled from this mill or brought in from the valley by wagon.

Adjacent to the sawmill are a number of spots where other buildings were located. One cabin is still standing. It is built in an "L" shape (Figure 41). It may have had a sleeping loft and probably served as a boarding house.

Upstream from the sawmill site is a large cabin (Figure 42). It was built on a stone foundation and is the only cabin located in all the drainages that was built in this manner. It consisted of four rooms, with one having wainscoting on the walls. It also had a brick chimney. The doors and windows were

Figure 39 – Steam engine in Willow Creek. It was used to power the sawmill at the head of the Willow Creek Flume. 2005. Parts of the sawmill are present along with scattered wagon parts. Photograph by B. John Losensky.

Figure 40 – Remains of a wagon axle found in the sawmill site in Willow Creek. 2005. PHOTOGRAPH BY B. JOHN LOSENSKY.

Figure 41 – Large L-shaped cabin at the sawmill site in Willow Creek. 2005. This was probably used as a boarding house for the workers. PHOTOGRAPH BY B. JOHN LOSENSKY.

Figure 42 – Large four-room cabin built on a foundation by the sawmill site in Willow Creek. 2005. Note the stone foundation under the structure. PHOTOGRAPH BY B. JOHN LOSENSKY.

commercially made, and the roof was covered with tin. This cabin may have been the home for Pearson. The area represented the headquarters for the logging operation.

One other settlement was in the West Fork Willow Creek (Map 11). West Fork Camp consisted of two separate groups of cabins. The group at the forks consisted of five cabins. The group farther south in the drainage consisted of at least four buildings. This site contained a horse barn, blacksmith shop, large company cabin for sleeping, and a cabin probably used as a boarding house (Figure 43). Other cabins found in the sale area are either single cabins or in groups of two or three and were probably used temporarily by the woodcutters when working in the area.

Other than the lack of trams, the logging methods were similar to those used by McCune. While McCune cut only firewood, the operation in Willow Creek made several products, including stulls, firewood, and lagging and converter poles, which were shipped to both Anaconda and Butte (Figure 44). Cutting was uncontrolled and was dependent on the whim of the logger.

With the establishment of the Forest Service in 1905, a new set of men were sent to manage the forests and control the unauthorized cutting of trees. Charges were brought against DeKay in 1906 by the Forest Service for taking 12,000 cords from Willow Creek without payment. He was charged $6,000, but letters between various governmental departments indicated they were doubtful that a case could be

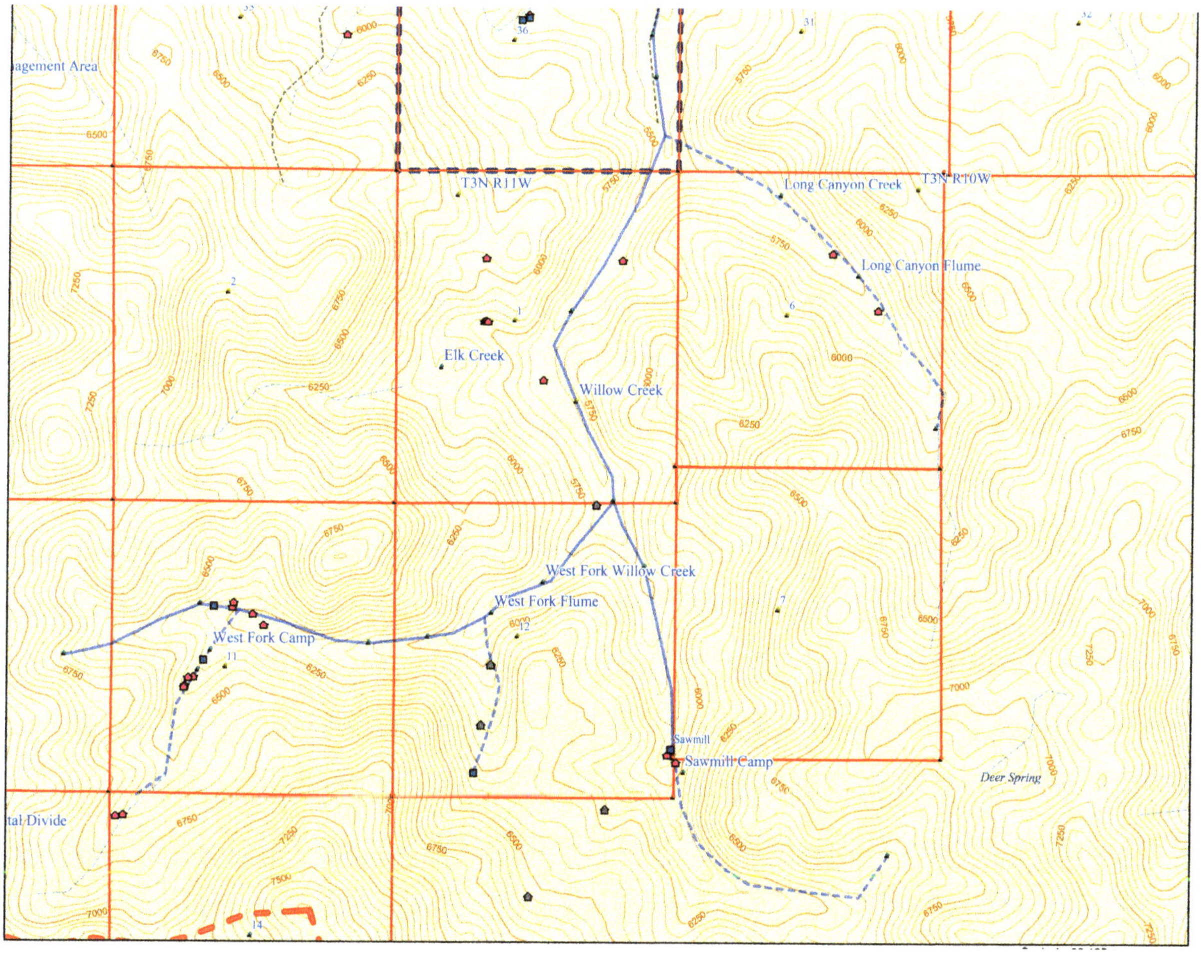

Map Legend

- Flume
- Flume not located
- Hoist tram
- Horse tram
- Cabin remains
- Cabin foundation
- Cabin shown on old maps not found
- Log chute
- Main road
- Forest access road
- Continental Divide
- Mt. Haggin WMA boundary
- Deerlodge-Beaverhead Forest boundary

Map 11 – Map of West Fork Camp and Sawmill Camp area.

Figure 43 – Company cabin in West Fork Willow Creek. 2004. PHOTOGRAPH BY B. JOHN LOSENSKY.

Figure 44 – Pile of lagging left in the West Fork Willow Creek. 2006. PHOTOGRAPH BY B. JOHN LOSENSKY.

won. Settlement of the issue was gained by DeKay when he provided his records to pursue a trespass case against A.W. McCune over a much larger trespass in Mill and Deep Creeks.[24]

This change in administration of the forest reserves also affected Pearson. On August 21, 1907, he received a contract from the Forest Service to log 24,205,000 board feet (bf) from the Big Hole National Forest. (The Willow Creek drainage was withdrawn from the public domain on November 5, 1906, and became part of the Big Hole Forest Reserve. It became a national forest on March 4, 1907, and on July 1, 1908, the forest was split into the Deerlodge and Beaverhead National Forests.[25]) It is unclear if this sale covered past cutting or future activity. Subsequently, Pearson contracted for seven additional sales in the Willow Creek drainage for an additional 6,144,000 bf. The last sale was closed on August 12, 1916, ending twenty-two years of logging in Willow Creek.[26] The total removed from the drainage by all the operators probably exceeded 80,000,000 bf.

CHAPTER THIRTEEN

A New Player

By the turn of the 20th century, changes were underway within the land management agencies in Washington. A push to remove timbered lands from disposal resulted in the creation of the forest reserves in 1891. They became the basis for the National Forest System. The Yellowstone Park Timberland Reserve was part of these lands and is now one of the keystone parks in the National Park System: Yellowstone National Park. Gifford Pinchot was one of the major proponents for forest management on the public domain.[1] He was born in 1865 to James and Mary Eno Pinchot of New York City. His father and grandfather were both in the timber business and had made a fortune buying land, cutting the timber, and then selling the cutover lands. Gifford grew up with the New York City elite, but rather than continue the business, he became interested in how to manage forest lands. He went to France to study forestry and upon his return was employed by George Vanderbilt to manage his estate in North Carolina in 1892. He became active in promoting changes in the management of the public domain. In 1894, he, along with Charles Sargent, William Stiles, and Robert Johnsen, developed a bill that would appoint a commission to report on the public timberlands. This bill did not pass, but Pinchot was able to get a commission appointed within the National Academy of Sciences to investigate the management of public timberlands. This commission recommended the establishment of thirteen forest reserves, which President Cleveland created, covering over twenty-one million acres in the western United States. While some of the public forest land was now no longer available for homesteads, illegal timber removal continued. Efforts to reduce timber theft from the reserves and the public domain lands gained support when Theodore Roosevelt, a good friend of Pinchot's, became president in 1901. The country now had a person in charge who took a strong interest in the nation's forests. In 1898, Pinchot became the head of the Bureau of Forestry. Between then and 1905, he worked tirelessly to introduce sound management practices on the forest reserves. Finally, on February 1, 1905, Pinchot was able to unify all Federal Forest administration under the Department of Agriculture's Bureau of Forestry, and the Forest Service was established a few months later on July 1, 1905. Political appointment of forest rangers came to an end and rangers were now required to meet certain qualifications. A new management philosophy directed rangers to halt uncontrolled harvest on the forest reserves.

Into this new management environment stepped William R. Allen. Allen was born in French Gulch, Montana, on July 25, 1871, where his father was one of the original locators of the gold mines there[2] (Figures 45–46). Allen attended school in Deer Lodge County and Helena Business College. For a short period of time he was also employed by Daly in the Electric Light, Street Railway, and Water Works Department of the Anaconda Company and was probably aware of the company's wood needs because of that employment. In 1898, he left that job and took over the French Gulch mining operation from his father. He acquired a significant number of the original claims from other miners and introduced hydraulic mining into the drainage. He apparently was highly successful in this venture.

Figure 45 – Town of French Gulch in 1908. Allen's store is shown in the lower center of the photograph. Photo courtesy of Vanna Boccadori at Mount Haggin Wildlife Management Area. Photographer unknown.

Figure 46 – W.R. Allen standing in front of the cabin where he was born in French Town. Early 1900s. Photograph courtesy of Vanna Boccadori at Mount Haggin Wildlife Management Area. Photographer unknown.

Figure 47 – Tent Camp and crew for Allen's operation in 1905. Photograph courtesy of Vanna Boccadori at Mount Haggin Wildlife Management Area. Photographer unknown.

Sometime in 1905 he became interested in entering the logging business near his mining interests at French Gulch. Despite not having a government contract, he started cutting timber that year to build an extension to the old McCune Flume from its crossing of the Continental Divide to the NE ¼ Section 4 T2N, R11W in American Creek (Map 12, Figures 47–54.)

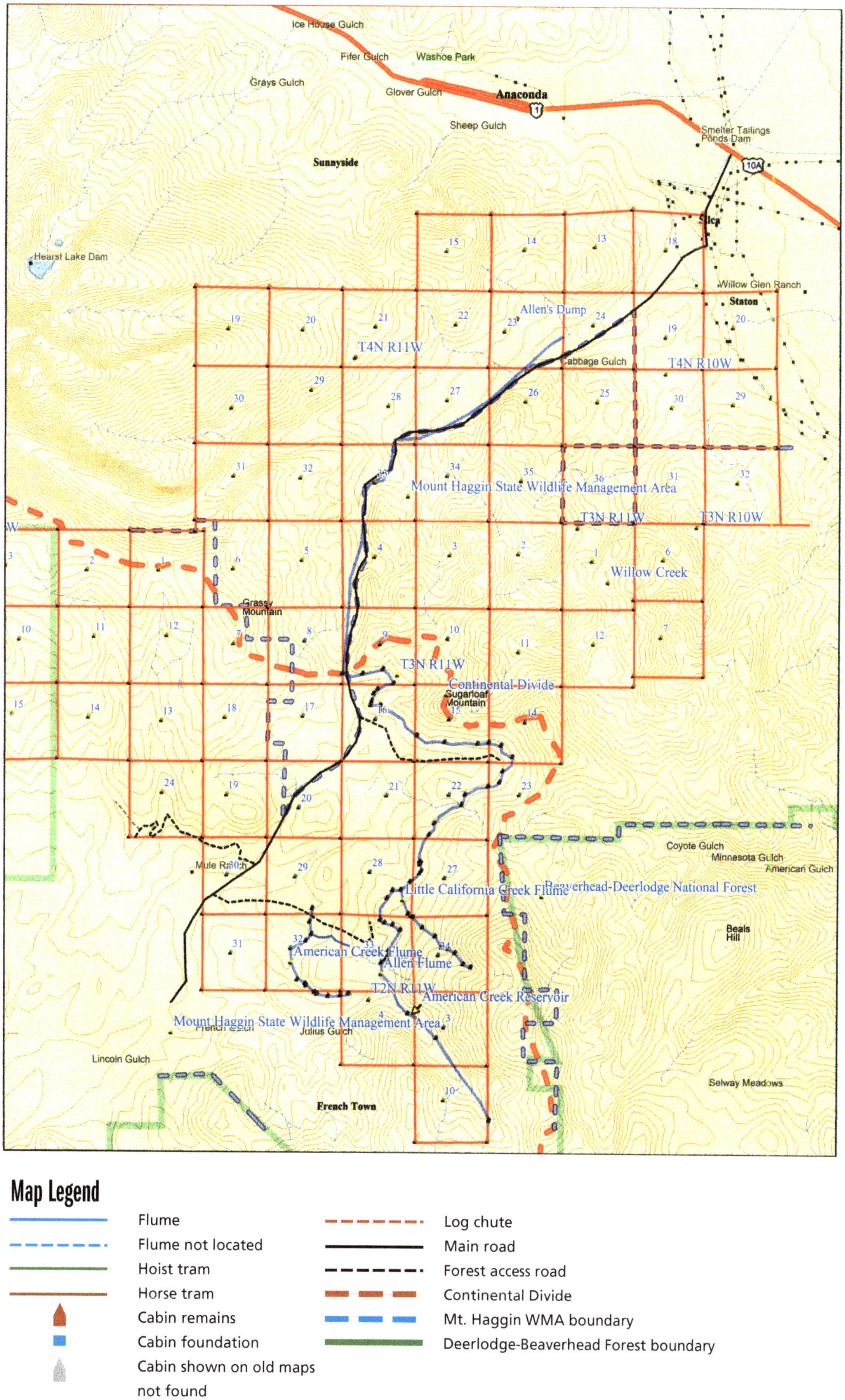

Map 12 – Allen's sale area map.

Figure 48 – Survey crew who located Allen's flume, ca. 1905. Sugarloaf Mountain in the background shows the results of McCune's logging with the slope clear-cut. Photograph courtesy of University of Montana Archives and Special Collections (77-146). Photographer unknown.

Figure 49 – Sawmill at Camp Two. 1900s sawmills like this were set up at various point along the path of the flume to produce lumber for construction of the flume. Photograph courtesy of National Archives RG-95-83933. Photographer unknown.

Figure 50 – Stacks of lumber produced at the mill located by the tram in Crooked John Creek, ca. 1908. The lumber was apparently moved up to the flume on the Crooked John Tram to construct the flume. Photograph courtesy of University of Montana Archives and Special Collections (77-161). Photographer unknown.

Figure 51 – Hand excavation of flume path through a ridge between the Continental Divide crossing and Sugarloaf Mountain. This area was cutover by McCune, ca. 1905. Photograph courtesy of University of Montana Archives and Special Collections (77-153). Photographer unknown.

Figure 52 – Constructing the flume, ca. 1905. The men are carrying prefab flume frames to extend the flume. Note the water overflow and stack of lumber floated down the flume in the construction process. Photograph courtesy of University of Montana Archives and Special Collections (77-147). Photographer unknown.

Figure 53 – Connection of Allen's Flume to McCune's Flume on the Continental Divide. McCune's Flume was blocked and bears off to the right. 1996. PHOTOGRAPH BY B. JOHN LOSENSKY.

Figure 54 – Remains of the flume west of Sugarloaf Mountain in the 1980s. Note the cabin in the upper right used by a flume tender. Heavy erosion has occurred with limited recovery. PHOTOGRAPH COURTESY OF VANNA BOCCADORI AT MOUNT HAGGIN WILDLIFE MANAGEMENT AREA. PHOTOGRAPHER UNKNOWN.

Allen's main flume was about ten miles long to where it connected to McCune's Flume on the Continental Divide and was completed in the fall of 1905. The sides of the flume were thirty-four inches, and the top was forty-seven inches wide. It was constructed with 1.5-inch boards.[3] Battens were placed over the cracks between the boards to reduce leakage.[4] In addition to the water added at its source in American Creek, there were five additional feeders before the flume crossed the Continental Divide and seven feeders between the Continental Divide and the "dump." The location of these feeders is vague in the record, but water was probably picked up from Little California, Crooked John, California, and an unnamed branch of California Creek near the Continental Divide. No locations were shown for the seven feeders in Mill Creek. The average grade between the head of the flume and the Continental Divide was about one and a half percent and, between the divide and the "dump," four percent. One tunnel 685 feet long was required in the construction (Figure 55).

Figure 55 – North end of the tunnel, which has caved in. 1996. PHOTOGRAPH BY B. JOHN LOSENSKY.

Figure 56 – "S" curve near Crooked John Creek, ca. 1906. Another example of the complex construction to maintain a constant grade. PHOTOGRAPH COURTESY OF UNIVERSITY OF MONTANA ARCHIVES AND SPECIAL COLLECTIONS (77-150). PHOTOGRAPHER UNKNOWN.

Figure 57 – Remains of the "S" curve trestle. Note the boardwalk along the side for the flume tenders. 1998. PHOTOGRAPH BY B. JOHN LOSENSKY.

In addition, there were twenty-nine trestles over twenty-five feet high, the highest being seventy-two feet and the longest 775 feet (Figures 56–57). It cost about $4,000 (about $135,400 in 2022 dollars) per mile to construct and and required 100,000 board feet of lumber per mile for construction[5] (Figures 58–59).

Figure 58 – Completed flume. 1906. Note the material cut for the right-of-way for the flume stacked and ready to float down the flume. Also note the telephone line running by the flume. This line extended from the "dump" to the town of French Gulch and provided communication among the various work sites and camps. PHOTOGRAPH COURTESY OF UNIVERSITY OF MONTANA ARCHIVES AND SPECIAL COLLECTIONS (77-152). PHOTOGRAPHER UNKNOWN.

Figure 59 – Flume dropping off the Continental Divide by the Anaconda-Ralston Road. 1900s. This area was logged earlier by McCune. Photograph courtesy of Vanna Boccadori atMount Haggin Wildlife Management Area. Photographer unknown.

Figure 60 – "Dump" at the end of Allen's flume with branches to separate material, ca. 1906-08. Note steam shovel used to load the cars. As the pile was built, sections of flume were added to the end and laid on top of the pile. These flume sections were also used to divert the material unto the various piles. Photograph courtesy of University of Montana Archives and Special Collections (77-192). Photographer unknown.

Allen rebuilt about six miles of the old McCune's Flume to reach the "dump" located at the horseshoe bend of the railroad near Mill Creek Station (Map 12, Figures 60–62).

Figure 61 – Hand loading firewood onto rail cars, ca. 1906-08. Photograph courtesy of University of Montana Archives and Special Collections (77-186). Photographer unknown.

Figure 62 – Hand-loading logs onto rail cars at the "dump," ca. 1908. Note the water from the flume being dumped on the ground to eventually make its way to Mill Creek. Photograph courtesy of University of Montana Archives and Special Collections (77-178). Photographer unknown.

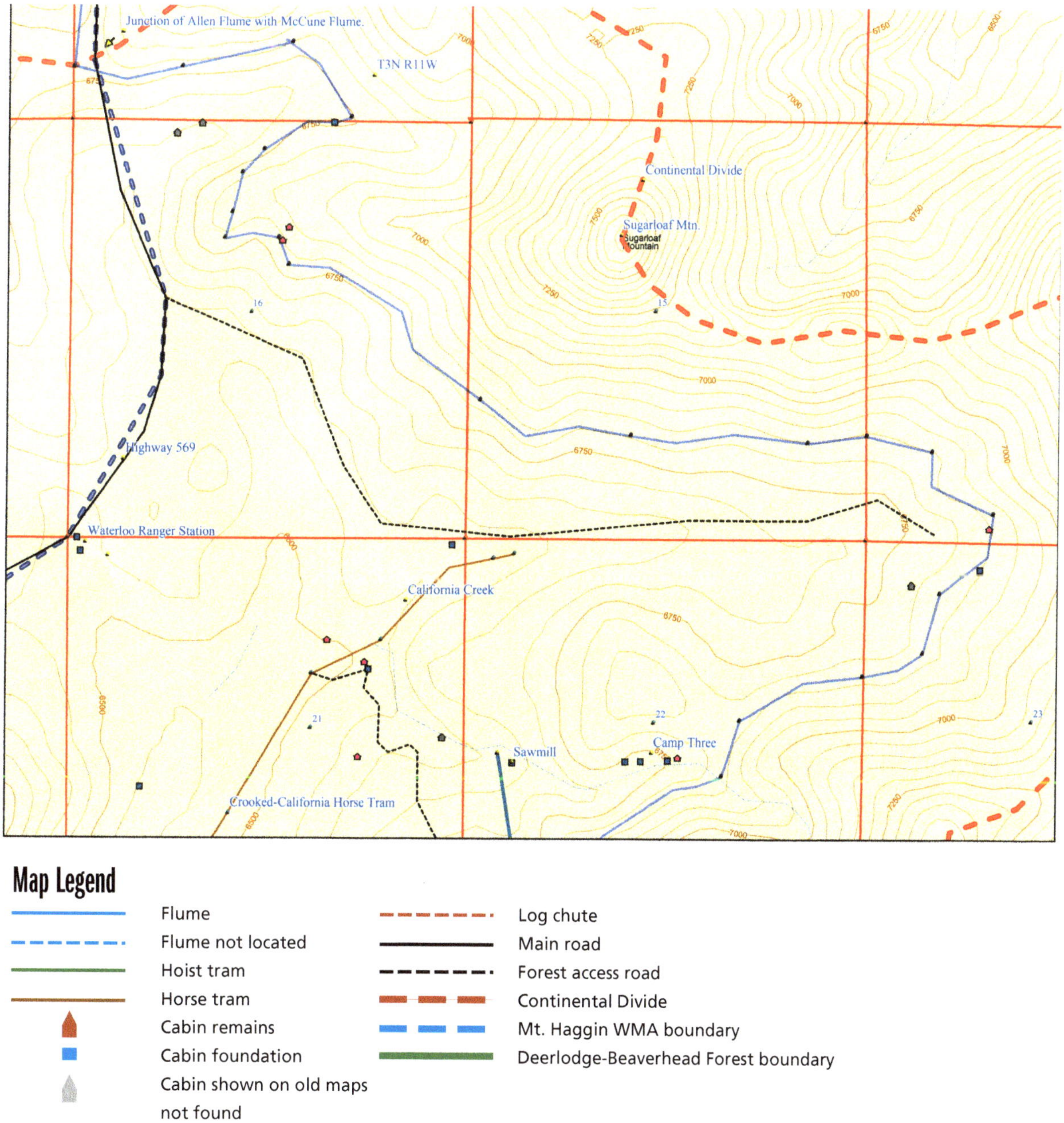

Map 13 – Map of Allen's flume from the Continental Divide to Camp Three area.

From the Continental Divide to near Camp Three, Allen crossed the old logging of McCune. McCune had logged the north side of the California Creek drainage (Map 13). From there the flume crossed into Crooked John Creek. Since much of the sale area was located below the flume, several trams were constructed to bring the material up to the flume in this drainage. The trams were unnamed, so to properly identify each tram, the author applied a name based on their physical location. The Bridge-Sawmill tram was located in Section 22 T3N, R11W (Map 14). It was about 2,475 feet long and gained about 320 feet in elevation. It started near the road bridge across the flume and ended near the sawmill in Spring Gulch [6] (Figure 63). It was probably first used to bring lumber to the flume during construction and later used in the logging operation. The Bridge-Crooked John Tram also started near the bridge over the flume in Section 22. It was about 4,285 feet long and gained about 410 feet in elevation. On the 1906 sale area map it is marked as the "old tram," and it ended in Crooked John Creek.[7] Here a horse tram went from this point up California Creek about 6,600 feet with a favorable grade of about one and a half percent. Material from the slopes was moved to this tram and then loaded on tram cars that were pulled by a horse to the bottom of the Bridge-Crooked John Tram, where they were hoisted to the flume (Figures 64–65). These trams were used in the logging between 1906 and 1908.[8]

Figure 63 – Bridge over flume by site of Bridge-Crooked John Tram. 1998. Remains of the flume can be seen in front of the bridge. PHOTOGRAPH BY B. JOHN LOSENSKY.

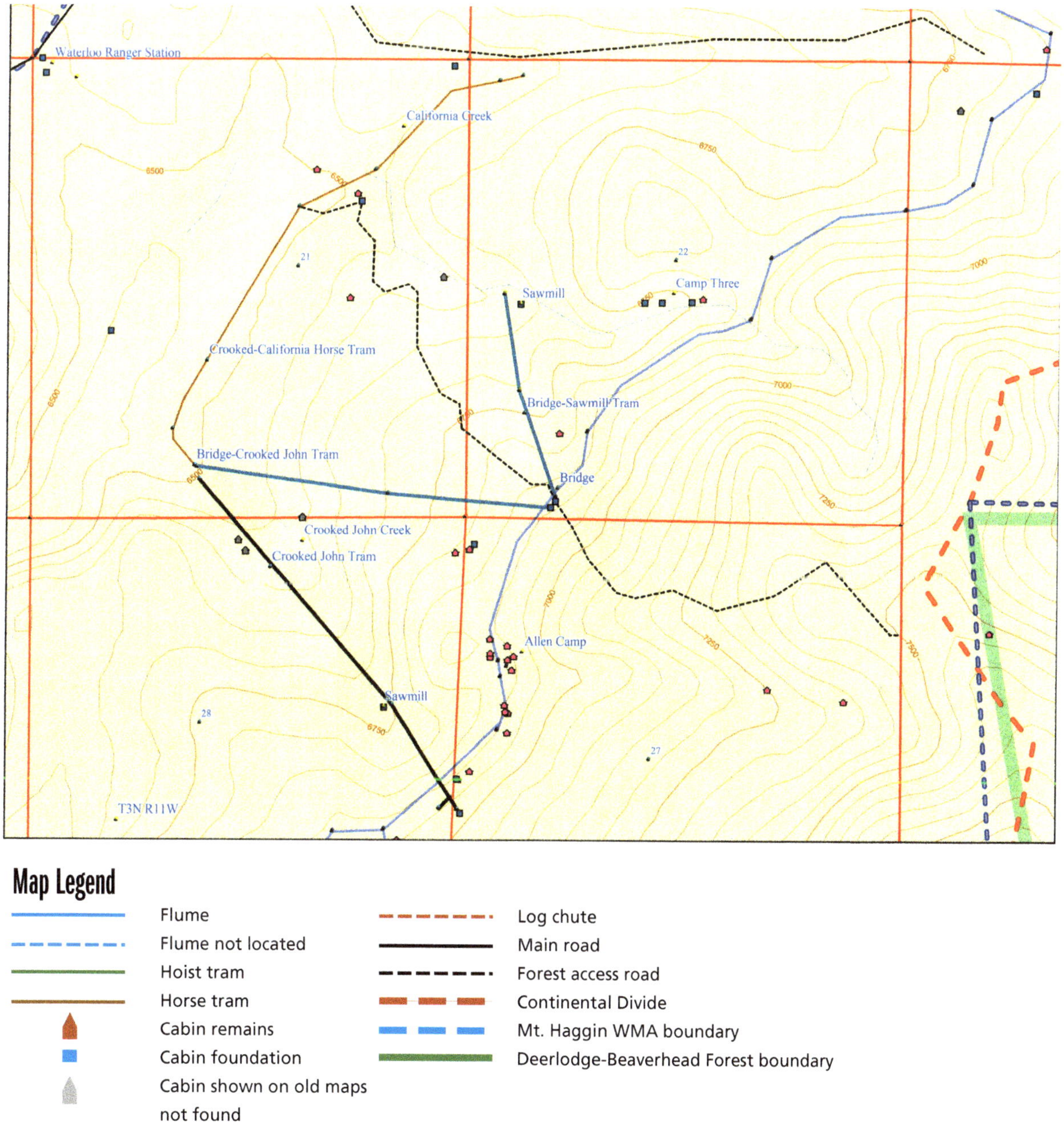

Map 14 – Map of Allen's Camp area showing the location of the three trams in Crooked John Creek and Spring Gulch.

Figure 64 – Top of the Bridge-Crooked John Tram, ca. 1906-08. The flume is just off the right side of the photograph. Material was decked above the flume and then fed into it by gravity. A loaded tram car is located just below the siding. Photograph courtesy of University of Montana Archives and Special Collections (77-189). Photographer unknown.

Figure 65 – Bridge-Crooked John Tram showing loading area. 1908. Note the flume running between the two workers. The top of the tram is by the horse where a siding runs parallel to the flume and material is stacked to feed the flume. Photograph courtesy of University of Montana Archives and Special Collections (77-174). Photographer unknown.

Figure 66 – Double landing at base of Crooked John Tram, ca. 1908. No evidence of the cabin in the photograph was found. Also note the tent camp up slope from the landing. A tram car is being pulled up to the flume and a second group of loaded cars waits at the end of the tram. PHOTOGRAPH COURTESY OF MILE HIGH NORDIC SKI EDUCATION FOUNDATION. PHOTOGRAPHER UNKNOWN.

Figure 67 – Little California flume. Note the small stream next to the remains of the flume. Large piles of cordwood were located above this picture that were not removed. 1996. PHOTOGRAPH BY B. JOHN LOSENSKY.

The Crooked John Tram is in Crooked John Creek and started in the SE ¼ Section 28 T3N, R11W (see Map 14, Figure 66). It is about 4,980 feet long and ended near the bottom of the Bridge-Crooked John Tram. It gained about 475 feet in elevation and was used primarily during the logging of 1908 and 1909.[9]

There was a sawmill adjacent to the tram in Crooked John Creek about halfway down the tram (see Figure 46).

The flume continued south, and a secondary flume went up Little California Creek (Figure 67). It was about one and a half miles long and on about an 11 percent grade. This stream had limited water, and the flume may have not seen much use.

The main flume continued through a tunnel and by Camp Two. Just beyond the camp was the Little American Creek Tram (Figure 16). It was built in December 1910. It started in the middle of Section 33 T3N, R11W and was 982 feet long[10] (Map 15). By 1912, the tram had been extended to about 6,600 feet[11] (Figure 11). It gained about 570 feet in elevation for a grade of about 9 percent.

E.W. Kramer, District Engineer for the Forest Service, studied the Little American Creek Tram on a day when there were eight cars in the train that was being raised and lowered on the tram. Fifteen logs were loaded on each car and eight men loaded the cars in about thirty minutes. It took eight minutes to raise the train from the end of the tram and about four minutes to lower it back again. The cars were unloaded in about eight minutes into piles by the flume. The hoist was operated with a 50-horsepower engine. Steam

Figure 68 – Landing at base of Little American Creek Tram. 1913. Nels Pearson is standing under one of the loading decks for the American Creek Flume. A second deck is behind him where a car is being loaded. Photograph Courtesy of Marcus Daly Museum & Archives. Photographer unknown.

was supplied to the engine from three boilers, and the system was operated by an engineer and one fireman.[12]

One of the main products produced in Allen's sale were stulls used in the mines. A study during winter logging found that it took one man sixteen minutes to make a stull. With two men working together, they could produce seventy stulls in a ten-hour day. The work was broken down into the following categories: shoveling snow, 15 percent; felling tree, 10 percent; trimming tree, 4 percent; piling and burning the slash, 16 percent; cutting the tree into stull length, 21 percent; and peeling stulls, 34 percent.[13]

A system of flumes from Little American Creek and American Creek ended at the base of this tram (Map 15, Figure 68). The American Creek Flume ran southerly across Little American Creek into American Creek. It continued up American Creek into the NW ¼ Section 4 T2N, R11W. It was about 1.75 miles long and had a 2 percent grade (Figure 69). A short flume about one half-mile long branched off this flume and ran up Little American Creek. It was on about a 5 percent grade. These flumes in the American Creek drainage were constructed after 1910, as they do not appear on the 1906 map. They do appear on the map showing cutting method between 1905 and 1912.[14]

Figure 69 – Remains of the secondary flume up American Creek. 2002. Photograph by B. John Losensky.

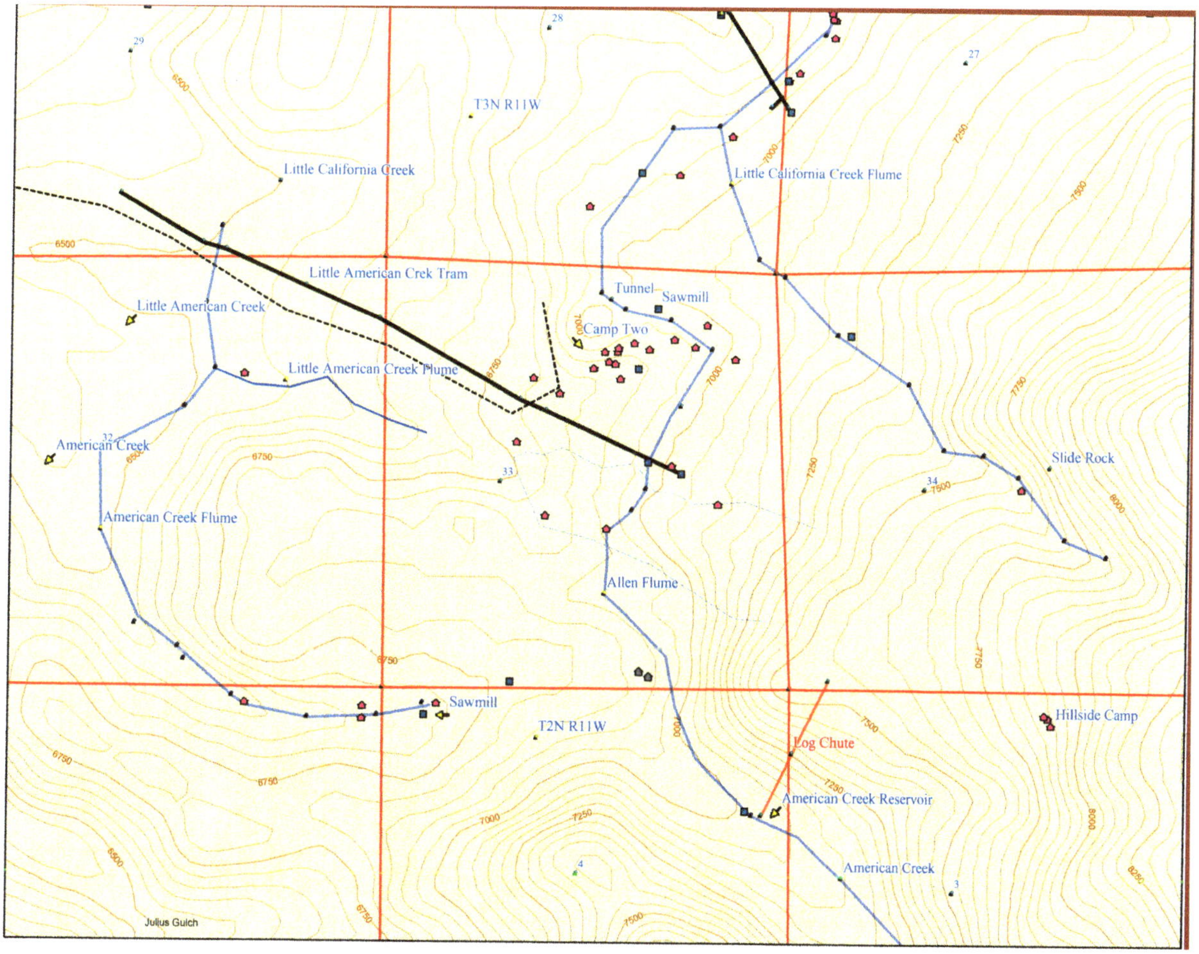

Map Legend

- Flume
- Flume not located
- Hoist tram
- Horse tram
- Cabin remains
- Cabin foundation
- Cabin shown on old maps not found
- Log chute
- Main road
- Forest access road
- Continental Divide
- Mt. Haggin WMA boundary
- Deerlodge-Beaverhead Forest boundary

Map 15 – Map of Camp Two and Little American Creek Tram and the system of secondary flumes associated with the tram.

In addition to the trams, there was one log chute which started in the NW ¼ Section 3 T2N, R11W and ended in the reservoir in American Creek (Map 16, Figures 70–72). It was about 1,870 feet in length and dropped about 520 feet for an average grade of about 28 percent. It probably was constructed about the same time as the Little American Creek Tram. Once the logs were in the reservoir, they were fed into the flume by a four-man crew. This same crew also had the contract to load the material into the chute and move it down the chute to the reservoir. At the time of Kramer's visit a price had not yet been determined for the work.[15]

The flume originally ended at the reservoir in American Creek. A map showing the sale progress between 1906 and 1910 shows the portion of the flume above the dam as new flume.[16]

Operating the flume required a great deal of water, as leaking was a continuing problem. Over time Allen had acquired water rights in First Chance Gulch, American Creek, California Creek, Julius Gulch, Fenian Gulch, and Spring Gulch. Some of these water rights were associated with Allen's mining operation. Apparently, Allen used the water rights held by the Anaconda Company for the flume north of the Continental Divide.

Figure 70 – Log chute and reservoir in American Creek. 1913. Remains of one of the two cabins were found. The reservoir is filled mainly with stulls. PHOTOGRAPH COURTESY OF MARCUS DALY MUSEUM & ARCHIVES. PHOTOGRAPHER UNKNOWN.

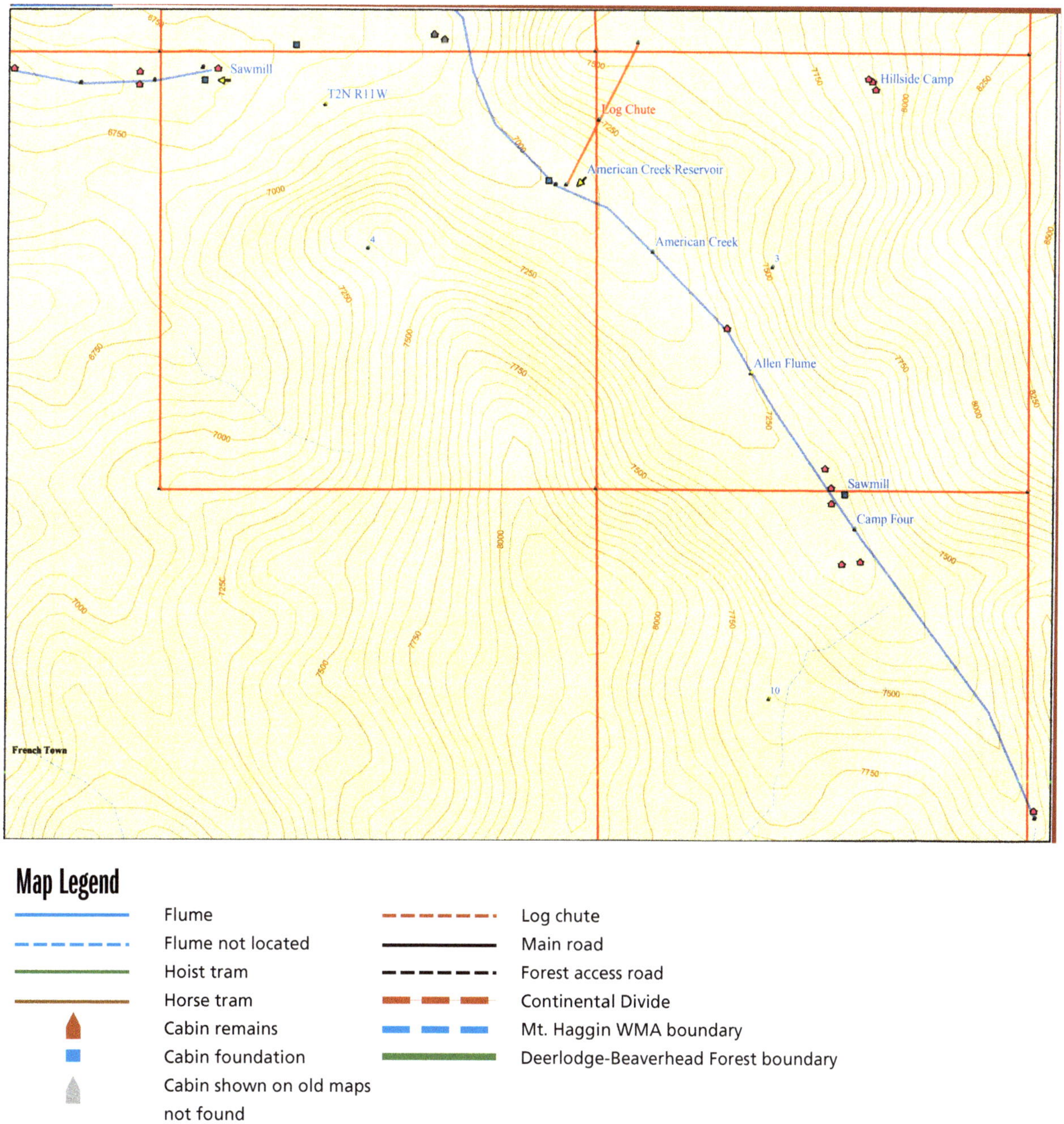

Map 16 – Map of Camp Four and the log chute and reservoir in American Creek.

Figure 71 – Upper portion of log chute into American Creek, ca. 1908. PHOTOGRAPH COURTESY OF UNIVERSITY OF MONTANA ARCHIVES AND SPECIAL COLLECTIONS (77-198). PHOTOGRAPHER UNKNOWN.

Figure 72 – Remains of log chute into American Creek. 1998. PHOTOGRAPH BY B. JOHN LOSENSKY.

CHAPTER FOURTEEN

Allen's Work Camps

During the life of the Allen sale, several settlements were developed either to support construction of the flume or for the logging operation. The old sale maps showed the location of some of these camps. Camp Three was in the middle of Section 22 T3N, R11W, adjacent to Spring Gulch (Map 13). This camp had only one remaining cabin when surveyed in 2004[1] (Figure 73). There were foundations for two barns and at least one other cabin. It probably was used when the sawmill located nearby was in operation.

Figure 73 – Camp Three cabin remains in Camp Three. It had a board roof and floor since it was near a sawmill. 1998. PHOTOGRAPH BY B. JOHN LOSENSKY.

Allen's Camp was located in Crooked John Creek (Map 14, Figure 74). It does not show on either of the old sale maps.[2] It is a much larger camp than the one in Spring Gulch; the maps may have been mislabeled. It was in the NE ¼ Section 28 T3N, R11W. There are remains of five cabins, two bunkhouses, and two barns in this camp. A sawmill was located adjacent to the tram in Crooked John Creek below the town site. This settlement was important during the operation of the three trams in the area.

Camp Two, or Main Camp, was in the NW ¼ Section 33 T3N, R11W and was the largest camp found on the sale area (Map 15). It contained at least seven cabins, three barns, three boarding houses, two sheds, one store, and a ranger station (Figures 75–78).

Figure 74 – View of Allen's Camp located in the upper reaches of Crooked John Creek. 2002. PHOTOGRAPH BY B. JOHN LOSENSKY.

Figure 75 – Boarding house in Allen's Camp Two. This was a two-story building with sleeping quarters on the upper floor, ca. 1980s. Photograph courtesy of Vanna Boccadori at Mount Haggin Wildlife Management Area. Photographer unknown.

Figure 76 – US brand in the end of a log of the boarding house in Camp Two. 2004. A branding hammer would have been used by the timber markers to indicate that the tree was to be harvested. Photograph by B. John Losensky.

Figure 77 – This was probably the Ranger Station in Allen's Camp Two. 1998. The interior walls were covered with shingles and the door had a window in it. It also had a flat roof sloping to the rear. These construction details make the cabin unique. Photograph by B. John Losensky.

Figure 78 – Skidding teams at Allen's Camp Two, ca. 1908. The large building on the right could be a store. Allen had about 200 head of horses and some mules to haul timbers on his sale.[3]
Photograph courtesy of University of Montana Archives and Special Collections. Photographer unknown.

Figure 79 – Sawmill at Camp Two, ca. 1908. Note the flume running behind the mill; at the far right it enters the tunnel. The camp was located downslope from the mill. Photograph courtesy of University of Montana Archives and Special Collections (77-169). Photographer unknown.

There was a sawmill located here, and, after the flume was built, additional lumber would have been required to make repairs on the flume during its life (Figure 79). This sawmill was listed as the "new mill" and may have replaced the one shown in Figure 49.

Camp Four was located at the head of the flume in the SW ¼ Section 3 T2N, R11W along American Creek (Map 16). This camp was at the end of the flume and contained the remains of five cabins, one bunkhouse, and a barn (Figure 80). There was a sawmill located here also. One other sawmill was located at the head of the flume in American Creek in the NE ¼ Section 5 T2N, R11W (Map 15) and probably was used to cut lumber for this secondary flume and the one in Little American Creek (Map 15). There was probably only one sawmill that was moved to the various places during construction of the flume.

Figure 80 – A large multi-room cabin located at Allen's Camp Four. 1998. This cabin has been maintained over time and used by hunters in the fall. PHOTOGRAPH BY B. JOHN LOSENSKY.

There are many other cabins scattered throughout the sale area in singles or small groups that were used in the logging operation. In addition to the Ranger Station at Camp Two, a station was also located adjacent to the Anaconda-Ralston Road in the SE ¼ Section 17, T3N R11W (Map 14). This location is shown as the 15-Mile House on the 1906 map and had been established by a French-Canadian man named Napoleon Tessier.[4] Tessier built his log cabin saloon and restaurant before the establishment of the Hell Gate Forest Reserve, which eventually became the Deerlodge National Forest. When the reserve was established, it was determined that he had an illegal claim and was required to close the operation. Tessier's loss was locally known as Napoleon's "Waterloo." After Tessier was evicted, the place was used as a ranger station and was referred to as the Waterloo Ranger Station. Tessier spent the rest of his life working at the Mule Ranch located a few miles away. He died in 1936 in St. Ann's Hospital in Anaconda.

CHAPTER FIFTEEN

Allen's Troubles

Allen cut about 10,000,000 bf of timber for construction of the flumes. In addition, he cut about 100,000 mining stulls, 6,000 cords of cordwood, 5,000 converter poles, 2,000 pieces of lagging, and 250,000 bf of sawtimber during the period from 1905 to early 1906.[1] However, little of this material was removed in 1905 or by the spring of 1906.[2] Allen assumed that the land was considered mineral and, as such, timber could be removed to support the mining activity. This cutting was going on at the same time the reserves were being transferred from the Department of Interior to the new Forest Service in the Department of Agriculture. In the spring of 1906, Special Agents H.H. Swartz and L.L. Sharp of the General Land Office (GLO) reported the cutting to the new Forest Supervisor E.A. Sherman of the Hell Gate Forest Reserve (later named the Deerlodge National Forest), and a restraining order was issued by the United States District Court of Montana enjoining Allen from further operations.[3] Recognizing that he could not win the case because of the change in land classification and administration, he offered to settle for the value of the timber and the damages sustained by the government. This early logging was unregulated and apparently left a mess on the ground. In an agreement dated June 11, 1906, Allen proposed a settlement for the timber he had cut in 1905.[4] Value of the various products on the ground were estimated at $2 per thousand board feet (mbf) for saw timber, $1.65 per cord for firewood, 22.4 cents each for stulls, 7 cents each for converter poles, 2.5 cents each for lagging, and $8.50 per mbf for fir (Douglas fir) saw timber. The marketplace for the material was listed as Butte for the cordwood and lagging, Rocker for mining stulls, and Anaconda for converter poles. However, in the final settlement, timber and stulls were paid at the rate of $2.00 per mbf, 50 cents for cordwood, 2.5 cents for converter poles, and 1 cent for lagging. It is unclear why the rates were changed. Allen also agreed to burn the slash created by this logging.[5]

Finally, on July 19, 1906, a timber sale was developed for 220 acres in California Gulch for 2,030,000 bf of mining stulls, 3,000 cords of cordwood, and an unestimated number of converter poles. Payment was to be made at the rate of $3 per mbf for timber and stulls, 50 cents for cordwood, and one half-cent for converter poles.[6] It was further stated that no timber could be removed before the area of the timber trespass was cleaned up. The trespass area later called "Sale No. 1" was finally approved by the Forest Service on November 10, 1906.[7] It was located in the California Creek drainage near the present-day cross-country ski parking lot. The new sale was important both to the mining industry and the Forest Service, as it provided assurance to the mining industry that they would be able to get the wood resources they needed for their operation, and it also softened some of the objections to the formation of the national forests at a time when its future was uncertain. On August 27, 1906, Allen reached an agreement with the

Northwest Coal Company of Butte, Montana, to sell them 10,000 cords of wood at $4 per cord on cars at the terminus of the wood flume.[8] Later, in the fall of 1906, Gifford Pinchot, the head of the Forest Service, and his staff visited the sale area with Allen to further gain local support for the National Forest System.[9]

On September 16, 1907, Allen was awarded a second contract from the Forest Service to harvest 100,000 cords from an area in the California, Little California, Crooked John, American, and Little American Creek drainages.[10] At about the same time, the Forest Service issued a Special Privilege Agreement to operate a wood flume which had already been constructed in 1905. The head of the flume was shown as the NE ¼ Section 4 T2N, R11W (Map 16). The Forest Service also issued agreements to operate a telephone line from the French Gulch Store along the flume to the forest boundary and a permit to construct and maintain a pasture of 640 acres in Section 31 T3N, R11W. This area was located south of the Mule Ranch along American Creek.[11] These agreements were initiated to formalize conditions that were already in place on the ground. As stated above, Allen's sales covered a variety of products, including mining timbers such as lagging used to support the roof of a mine tunnel and stulls to support the lagging, along with converter poles used in the smelting operation and cordwood. Based on evidence on the ground, there may have been more cordwood in the sale area than he could sell, and significant amounts of cordwood can still be found throughout the area that was cut and stacked but not removed. There are several large piles representing hundreds of cords of wood at the head of Little California Creek that may have been left because of the lack of water to flume the material[12] (Figures 81–82).

Stacks of other products such as lagging and converter poles are also found throughout parts of the sale area (Figure 83). These piles could be signs of poor onsite management which contributed to Allen's continued problems of being in arrears with his payments.

By 1908, this problem resulted in the threat to close the operation until payment was made to the Forest Service. Allen requested an extension to January 1, 1909, to make payment of $32,000 that he owed for timber cut but not paid for. The Forest Service was reluctant to close the operation for fear of the potential impact on the survival of the National Forest System. They complied with Allen's request, and he was required to make monthly payments of $5,000 toward the deficit until it was paid off.[13] About the same time, Allen apparently attempted to sell the operation to some interests in Chicago, Illinois. In a letter dated October 1, 1908, it states he owed $26,000 for labor and $32,000 in stumpage that was not listed in the original report to the potential buyers and that this additional

Figure 81 – Stack of firewood left in Allen's sale. 1998. Stacks like this were found scattered throughout the sale area. Either the market for firewood was limited or they were missed in the skidding operation. Photograph by B. John Losensky.

Figure 82 – One of several piles of firewood left at the head of the flume in Little California Creek. 1999. This material may have been left because there was not enough water to float the material down the flume. Mistakes such as this may have contributed to Allen's financial problems. PHOTOGRAPH BY B. JOHN LOSENSKY.

Figure 83 – Stack of lagging in American Creek left by Allen. PHOTOGRAPH BY B. JOHN LOSENSKY.

amount plus other liabilities was not covered by the value of the timber on hand. Consequently, the buyers were unwilling to take over the company because of this indebtedness. In the statement of assets, Allen listed the following products at the flume "dump": 68,674 stulls, 30,815 converter poles, 5,745 cords of cordwood, and 48,354 lagging poles. In addition, there were an estimated 207,840 stulls, 10,819 cords of wood, 73,452 converter poles, and 247,924 lagging poles cut but not flumed. The total value for the timber was listed as $147,513 ($4,777,950 in 2022 dollars).[14]

While the Forest Service was intent on providing sound management for the forest reserves, they also faced several problems in the administration of the sale. There was a lack of trained foresters to take charge of operations and the new rangers had to learn on the job. Secondly, there was little information available on how to manage lodgepole pine, which dominated the area. These problems are highlighted in a letter from Samuel Gross.[15] He was an employee of the Forest Service who worked on the sale in 1908. He was responsible for measuring the products cut to determine what Allen owed. He complained that logging was scattered over the whole area and was not being managed in a businesslike manner. He felt the trespass area known as Sale 1 should never have been accepted, as it was not properly done. He noted that the selection cutting method was a failure, as the remaining trees were falling down. This memo was sent to the Forester (now the Chief of the Forest Service) along with a cover memo from C.C. Hall Forest Supervisor countering some of Gross's statements. Mr. Hall states, "*Practically all the marking on this sale*

Figure 84 – A clear-cut unit in Allen's Forest Service sale. 1906–08. Note the stacks of firewood and log material used in the mines. PHOTOGRAPH COURTESY OF UNIVERSITY OF MONTANA ARCHIVES AND SPECIAL COLLECTIONS (77-159). PHOTOGRAPHER UNKNOWN.

was done in 1906 and was the first work done in marking, and the greater part of the cutting, brush piling, etc., was done in the latter part of 1906 and the first part of 1907 when the work was new." He also states, "*Taking into consideration that three or four changes have been made in the men handling this sale in the last two years, and that men without scarcely any previous experience in timber sale work have been in charge (for want of properly trained men) I am of the opinion that it has been very creditably handled, and a great improvement made over the first work.*"

Allen's contract was one of the largest in the United States under government supervision. Because of the lack of trained men, Allen claimed the Forest Service used his sale as a testing ground to determine cutting methods and to train men in the application of these procedures (Figures 84–85). He felt this put an additional burden on his operation.[16] By January 1909, Allen still owed $22,000 of the $32,000 deficit and again asked for an extension of time to May 1, 1909, to make the payment and permit him to continue cutting.[17] The extension was again approved, and logging continued.

Figure 85 – A unit in Allen's Forest Service sale where leave strips were left in the cutting unit, ca. 1908. This practice was dropped because of blowdown to the leave trees. PHOTOGRAPH COURTESY OF UNIVERSITY OF MONTANA ARCHIVES AND SPECIAL COLLECTIONS (77-157). PHOTOGRAPHER UNKNOWN.

In November of 1909, Allen took a group of thirty-three people on a tour of the operation, including Forest Supervisor C.C. Hall. After visiting the "dump" at the end of the flume they proceeded to French Gulch in eight automobiles, where Allen served them a splendid dinner. He then showed them the sawmill and planer mill which were operating there. They then took wagons up to Little American Creek Tram and watched them bring wood to the flume.[18] This trip was no doubt undertaken to promote his operation to the people of Anaconda.

Unfortunately, financial difficulties continued to plague the company and the Forest Service cancelled the contract on August 4, 1910. Allen again applied for an extension of time on August 7, 1910, which was approved yet again.[19] On November 8, 1910, despite his past failures to keep current on payments, the Forest Service sold him an additional 100,000,000 board feet in the same general area as his past sales.[20] The Forest Service was faced with a difficult situation. It was important for the agency to continue the sales, as there was a very real fear in the corporate world that the forest reserves would be locked up and they would not have a source of wood. Since there was a great deal of opposition to the reserves from other user groups, failure to continue to sell wood could cause Congress to disband the reserves. Consequently, the Forest Service felt compelled to work with Allen and attempt to keep the contracts going. It was plain to the Anaconda Company that if Allen continued to oversee their wood supply, they were in danger of losing it, so talks began for the company to buy out Allen and put a more reliable person in charge.

Meanwhile, logging continued with about sixty-five wood choppers employed working between Slide Rock in Little California Creek and the head of American Gulch.[21] Slide Rock got its name from the very large talus slopes on the northeast side of Little California Creek (Map 15). Later, in the winter of 1911, it was reported that seventy-five choppers plus a good-sized crew were working in one of the areas of fire-killed timber.[22] (Was this burn the one reported in 1889 that threatened French Gulch? See page 109.) It was noted in the *Anaconda Standard* on February 19, 1911, that the choppers had moved from the Slide Rock slope because of deep snow. (See Appendix D for a list of workers working on the sale area in 1910.) Cutting was delayed for a period by striking workmen, but the issue was soon resolved. The article also mentioned that 120,000 board feet of lumber had been cut to extend the American Gulch (Creek) Flume in the spring. (It is unclear if this was part of the main flume or the secondary flume in American Creek.) They were also constructing the dry chute into the reservoir in American Gulch.[23]

Negotiations continued between the Anaconda Company and Allen. In a letter dated March 30, 1911, John Ryan of the Anaconda Company indicated a willingness to take over Allen's Company, but he was unwilling to pay anything for it except the cost of Allen's debts.[24] At the same time, negotiations apparently were ongoing with the group in Michigan to purchase the company.[25] The Michigan deal was to pay $200,000 to cover the costs of Allen's debts and buy the stock of the company for ten cents a share. However, they wanted a year to finalize the deal. Apparently, this delay was not acceptable to Allen.

Then a letter dated April 4, 1911, set forth a proposal by the Anaconda Copper Mining Company to take over Allen's operation.[26] In the agreement, Allen would convey to the new company the following properties:

1. A group of mining claims including the Lone Star Lode, Esther Lode, Eureka Lode, and French Gulch Lode. It would also include what is known as the Home Camp (French Gulch town) of the Allen Company (Map 17).

2. All the waters and water rights from First Chance Gulch, American Gulch, California Gulch, Julius Gulch, Fenian Gulch, and Spring Gulch used by the Allen Company.
3. A timber flume along with all flume extensions, spurs, and platforms at the flume yards at Mill Creek; all railroad tracks, buildings, and machinery; and all camp buildings and cabins. All wood at what is known as Home Camp and the timber along the flume line and at the flume "dump."
4. All merchandise stock, office furniture, and rights of way for wagon roads.
5. The telephone line—including all telephones which runs from the flume yard to the store of the company and the camps of the company.
6. All timber growing on the mining claims that was to be sold to the French Gulch Mining Company.

The new company would pay Allen $178,000 to pay debts and liabilities of the Allen Company and pay the remaining debt to the Forest Service of $5,874.55 for the trespass case.

Allen agreed with the proposal and requested a transfer of the sale to a company to be formed by the Anaconda Copper Mining Company to complete the sale.[27] This solution was acceptable to Forest Supervisor David T. Mason.[28] A letter dated April 15, 1911, was sent to the Forester (Chief of Forest Service) requesting approval of closing the sales with Allen and reselling the sales to a company backed by the Anaconda Copper Mining Company.[29] The District Forester (today's Regional Forester) stated:

> *In my opinion the Service has everything to gain in the transfer of this contract, since the Allen Company has repeatedly failed to make payments due, and yet, due to the relation of the sale to the Butte market and the amount of capital tied up by the Allen Company, we have felt it would be unjust to close them down when they have failed to come up to the terms of the contract. This has made necessary repeated modifications of contract and general unsatisfactory conditions in the sale, so far as payments are concerned.*

It was recommended that the Allen sale contract expire automatically with the execution of a new contract prepared for the new operating company, it being identical to the present contract.[30] It was felt that the sale should not be opened to bid since the only access to the timber was through the flume owned by the Allen Company. The Deerlodge National Forest agreed and stated that after the payment of $5,874.55 that Allen owed, they would close the sale and make a new sale to the new company covering the same area as Allen's sale. This arrangement was agreed to at the national level and, with the formation of the Mines Timber Company backed by the Anaconda Company, a new sale was approved by the Forest Service on May 11, 1911.

After losing his logging company, Allen became involved with politics and development of the Elkhorn silver claims he owned in Brundy (changed to Coolidge), Montana. In 1913, he established the Boston and Montana Development Company to build a railroad to Coolidge to develop his mine. His wife died in 1917 and he remarried Ethel deMar in Boston, where he had moved. The mining effort was again a financial failure and finally fell victim to the Depression in the 1930s. In 1940, he came out of retirement to run for Congress, but was defeated by Jeannette Rankin in the Republican primary. He died on October 31, 1953.[31]

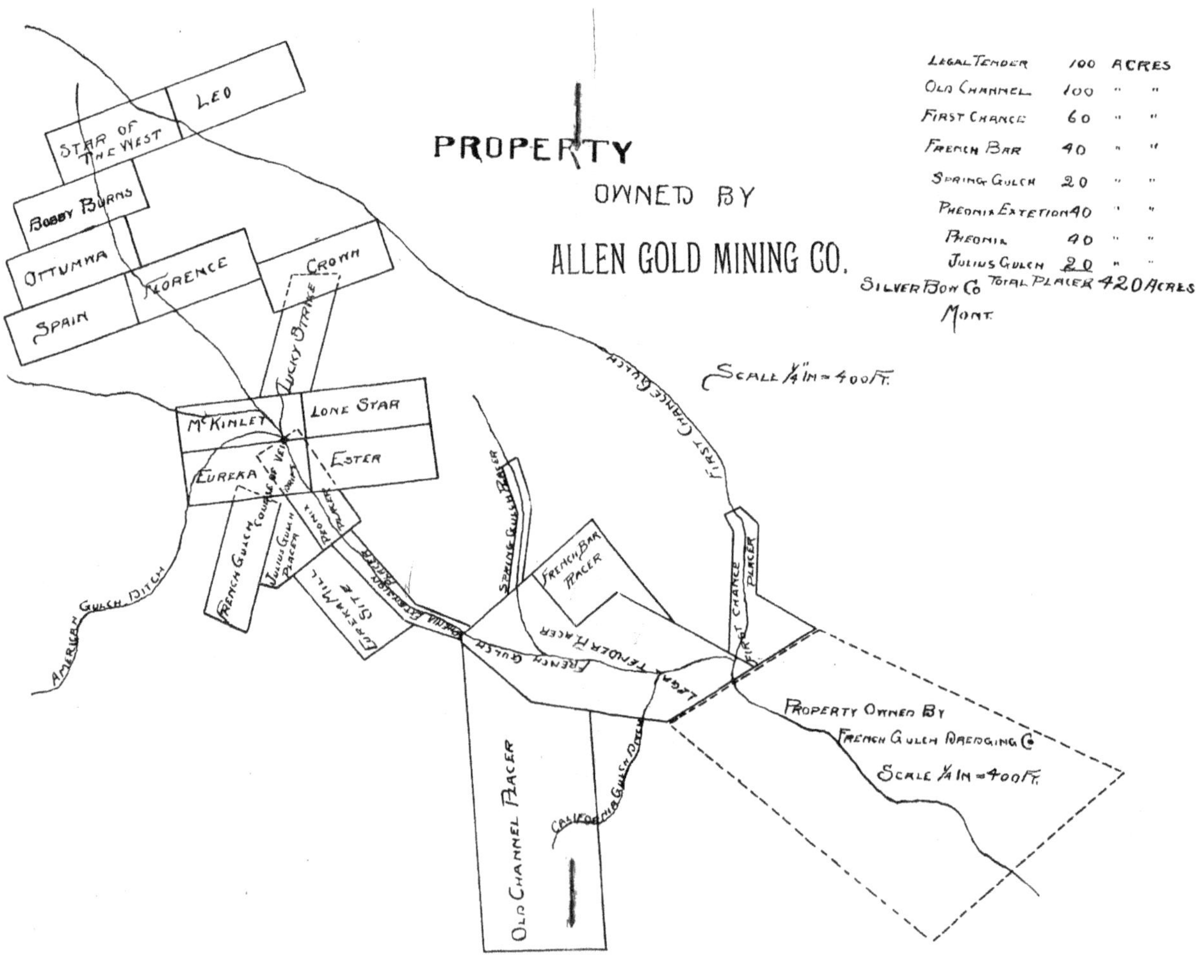

Map 17 – Map of the mining claims owned by Allen in the French Gulch area. From Allen Gold Mining Company, pages 8–9, 1903?

Upon completion of the transfer, Allen was removed from management and Nels Pearson was brought in to manage the operation. He was offered $15,000 a year (about $470,550 in 2022 dollars), a seven-passenger Stevens-Duryea car, and all expenses to live in French Gulch.[32] This change was noted in the *Anaconda Standard* on June 7, 1911.[33] He was provided a house in Frenchtown that may have been owned by the Mines Timber Company. From this camp he could drive to the various sites in the sale area where active logging was occurring. With the transfer to the Mines Timber Company, logging continued smoothly under Pearson and little news was recorded in the local papers. An article in the *Anaconda Standard* on December 14, 1913, stated that 400 men were employed in logging the area, along with 200 horses and several mules.[34] Because of the high cost of maintaining the flume and a limited operating period, building a railroad to the site was considered, but this option was not investigated further.[35]

Part of Allen's sale included Julius Gulch, where the town of French Gulch was located. The flume did not service this area and the material may have been milled at the sawmill in French Gulch. It is unclear if this lumber was then used locally or if it was hauled to Anaconda. A road did exist between French Gulch and the end of the lower flume on American Creek; the lumber could have been hauled by wagon to this flume and floated to the "dump."[36]

Between 1906 and 1913, the following products were removed from the sale area and floated down the flume: stulls, 1,286,000; cords of wood, 32,700; converter poles, 307,200; lagging, 633,000; and 157,700 coal props.[37] An adjustment was made on this contract on December 29, 1916, to modify utilization requirements and then a memo dated September 20, 1917, signed by District Forester Ferdinand A. Silcox closed the sale, thereby ending thirty-three years of flume logging in the French Gulch-Mill Creek area.[38]

CHAPTER SIXTEEN

Fire in the Woods

One of the most serious threats faced by the wood contractors was fire. The logging procedure used at that time resulted in firewood or logs being piled in the woods for an extended period, during which it was vulnerable to a fire. In some cases, if the wood had not been scaled (measured for payment), the woodchopper could lose a whole year of work and not get paid. Damage to the flumes that carried the wood was also a continual threat. Consequently, some of the earliest efforts to fight forest fires were undertaken by the logging community. Newspapers of the time reported on the fires and were a strong voice in getting the government to take action to control them. Not only were lightning and natural fires a problem, but also more serious man-caused fires. Woodchoppers living in the woods used primitive fireplaces or stoves for cooking and heating, making sparks a continual problem. A fire that threatened wood banked in the Elk Park north of Butte is an example. The *Semi-Weekly Miner* reported that a strong wind carried sparks from a woodchopper's cabin and ignited the slash on the ground. It burned for some time before the woodchopper, who was cooking dinner, discovered it.[1] Fortunately, the fire did not destroy any of the cut wood. However, the paper did note that it would impact the community in the future, as the burned timber was unfit for use as fuel.

The fire season of 1886 began early and lasted well into fall. A fire was reported raging near Butte in the Highlands in May.[2] Later that summer a fire hit the Caplice and McCune wood camp in Mill Creek. It was apparently started by a smoker who threw a lighted match. It burned about 500 cords of wood that had not been piled and accepted, so the woodchoppers lost out. The paper reported that two hundred men fought the fire for a day and a half.[3] In August, the *Semi-Weekly Inter-Mountain* reported that timber fires were common over all the territory and that Butte was in a smoky haze. There also was a big fire raging in the mountains east of Philipsburg, causing the Deer Lodge Valley to be full of smoke.[4] It was reported that all the employees of the mines at Granite and Philipsburg were fighting forest fires in that vicinity.[5] This fire was still burning on the 29th of August, and the *Semi-Weekly Inter-Mountain* stated that "*on Sunday night it presented a grand appearance to its spectators, lighting up the valley. East for miles. The smoke is very disagreeable.*"[6]

Fires continued to take their toll, and in September it was reported that 4,000 cords of wood were destroyed in Brown's Gulch near Butte. The wood had been piled by the flume, but there was not enough water to float the material, so the cut wood was to be flumed with the spring runoff. The stacks were ignited in several places and 500 feet of the flume was also burned for an estimated loss of $10,000 (about $317,000 in 2022 dollars)[7].

In October 1886, a large wood pile at the mouth of Silver Bow Canyon belonging to the Colorado Smelting Company was set on fire and nothing could be done to save the wood. There were ten freight cars on the sidetrack near the pile that also burned. The heat was so great that it warped the railroad tracks. It was estimated that 33,000 cords of wood were in the stacks, with an estimated value of $100,000 (about $3,170,000 in 2022 dollars).[8] The paper reported: *"A reward of $4,000 is offered for the arrest and conviction of the guilty parties, and it is hoped that the liberal sum will bring the dastardly offenders to justice."*[9] There was no follow-up story indicating that the arsonist was ever caught.

There was little activity reported for the next few years until the summer of 1889. The 1889 fire year probably burned more acres and was more widespread than the fires of 1910.[10] It has not gained as much interest, as no major towns were burned and loss of life was limited. On August 10, 1889, the *Semi-Weekly Miner* reported that while the fires had been raging for three weeks west of Butte, no one seemed to know much about where they are burning. F.R. Miles and John Corroll of the Jerry Creek Fluming Company went to investigate, since they had about 20,000 cords of wood cut in the general direction of the suspect fire. They discovered that the fire had started in Fish Trap Creek in a camp of tie-cutters and had burned into La March Creek, where it burned a dam belonging to the Big Hole Lumber Company. From there the fire had traveled in a northeast direction toward McCune's operation. They had a crew fighting the fire and had made some progress in checking its advance. Another fire had started in a tie-camp on the opposite side of Fish Trap Creek and burned a strip south and east for over twenty-five miles. A third fire was burning in the Dewey's Flat area of the Big Hole River near Wise River, Montana, and was burning west toward the Bitter Root Range.[11]

By August 21st, the town of Philipsburg was threatened, and men from the Butte area went to help fight the fire. Strong winds had pushed the fire within six miles of the town. The smoke around Butte was exceedingly dense from these fires.[12] On August 23rd, a fire was burning in Mill Creek, where it destroyed six miles of the Clear Creek Flume, a mile of the Mill Creek Flume, and about 500 cords of wood lying near the flume. McCune's crew was able to get it under control.[13] The situation continued to deteriorate, and on August 31st the *Semi-Weekly Miner* reported:

> *The high wind this afternoon brought the forest fire, which had been burning the past two days to the town side (*Anaconda*) of the hills immediately south of town. There has never been such high wind as that of today and there were some fears that it might bring it to the city, but the wind died away. . . . About 2,000 cords of wood belonging to different men in small lots was burned . . . a fire also started in French Gulch about 10 this morning and it is feared it will reach the Anaconda Fluming Company camp where they have over 75,000 cords of wood. Over 100 men have gone already to the camp and another large force will go up in the morning.*[14]

Fires continued to burn through September, with fire damaging the Black Pine Mine northwest of Philipsburg and another fire burning a strip two to four miles wide and fifteen miles long in the Bloody Dick Creek area southeast of Dillon, Montana.[15] Finally, on September 15th, the *Anaconda Standard* reported the fires around Philipsburg were under control, and on September 30th a fire near Philipsburg was put out by the rain.[16] The last fire reported in the papers for 1889 burned a large quantity of firewood in an immense fire east of Warm Springs Station, which was probably arson.[17]

After the fires of 1889, little fire activity was reported until October of 1890, when a fire near Butte burned a path seven or eight miles long and four to five miles wide. Damage was limited as the area had been logged eight years earlier.[18] About 500 cords of wood belonging to a group of Frechmen and Swedes were lost.

While fires continued to plague the logging industry in following years the area near McCune's, Allen's and the Willow Creek operations were relatively fire free until 1899, when a fire was reported southwest of Anaconda that destroyed 5,000 acres.[19]

In 1900, the head of Mill Creek burned primarily in old logging slash and the men from the French Gulch Placer mines went to fight it. Portions of the Mill Creek Flume were burned, but the flume was not in operation at that time.[20] A fire south of Anaconda was reported in August 1901, but apparently it did not attract much attention. By the middle of August that year, two fires were burning west of Anaconda. It was reported that Allen lost a large amount of corded wood. At one point there was concern that the flume would be burned and a crew of sixty men was sent out by Anaconda Copper Mining Company to fight the fire. Fortunately, the wind shifted, and rain put out the fires.[21] In 1901, a fire near Mount Haggin burned a large amount of cordwood that was stored there for the winter.[22] The area burned again the following year with considerable timber burned.[23]

The fires of 1910 by and large missed the area, but, considering the amount of logging and the number of past fires, the area that could sustain a large fire was limited. It was reported that on Allen's operation the efficient fire-fighting service saved all but a small part of the timber.[24] The town of Anaconda experienced heavy smoke from the fires burning in western Montana. It was reported that it was necessary to turn on the lights indoors before six o'clock.[25] A fire in Elk Park near Butte caused some concern and a call for 500 men was made to fight the blaze.[26] The 1910 fire season was the last major fire year reported in the Butte-Anaconda area prior to the end of the fluming operations in Mill and Deep Creek drainages. By this time, most of the major forest areas adjacent to Anaconda and Butte had either been logged or burned and, other than fires burning in the left-over slash, the impact of fire was limited for the next few decades.

CHAPTER SEVENTEEN

Living in the Woods

Because of the distance from town to the logging site, it was necessary for the wood workers to live at the work site. During the flume construction phase, a sawmill would be set up on the route of the flume near a stand of larger trees such as Douglas fir or spruce that could be used to make lumber. Sometimes tents were set up or cabins were built nearby to house the workers. These camps initially were used for only a short period until construction on that section of flume was completed. Because of the availability of lumber cut by the sawmill, boards were used for floors and roofs in these camps. The camps were commonly used later when logging occurred in the area. The cabins commonly were well-built, although there were exceptions (Figure 86). Once the logging began, the type of cabin and quality of construction was determined by considering how long the cabin would be used.

Figure 86 – Not all cabins were perfectly built. 2004. The wall of this cabin in Willow Creek needed to be braced after construction. This problem may have been the result of a heavy snow year. PHOTOGRAPH BY B. JOHN LOSENSKY.

Woodchoppers normally lived in small cabins near their job site alone or in small companies. Typically, simple cabins were built by the woodchoppers, since they may be used for only one season. At some point it was determined that the work site was too far from the cabin and a new cabin would be built at the current work area. These cabins were found singly or in small groups scattered through the logged area. Generally, they had dirt floors, and the roof was constructed with poles covered with dirt. The most common size was twelve feet by twelve feet, or about 144 square feet.[1] Some men worked together and would build a larger cabin that could house four or more people as shown in Figures 87–89.

Figure 87 – Cabin used by the crew of the Crooked John Tram. 1999. Logs were flattened on the inside and it had a wood floor. The remains of a shed are nearby along with the parts of a spring wagon. PHOTOGRAPH BY B. JOHN LOSENSKY.

Figure 88 –Interior of a cabin with wood floor near the Crooked John Tram in Allen's sale. 1998. This was a well built cabin with a wood floor and pole roof. Note the wood chinking between the logs. This cabin was used when the Crooked John Tram was in use. PHOTOGRAPH BY B. JOHN LOSENSKY.

Figure 89 – A company of woods workers employed on Allen's sale, ca. 1908. The gentleman on the right may be a visitor based on his dress. Photograph courtesy of University of Montana Archives and Special Collections (77-203). Photographer unknown.

The flume tender was assigned about a two-mile section of flume to maintain, and their cabins were located by that section of flume. These cabins were typically used for the life of the operation and frequently were of more substantial construction. Board roofs and wood floors were more common and small storage sheds often present.

Small settlements developed near the trams; cabins found there were typically more substantial. Commonly, a boarding house was associated with these locations (Figures 75 & 90). These provided a place to

Figure 90 – This is an example of a cabin probably used as a mess hall or boarding house. 2001. It is 22x55 feet and has two rooms with a log wall between them. It had six windows and three doors and is located at Corral Tram Camp in the McCune cutting (Map 8). Photograph by B. John Losensky.

sleep and provided meals for the men. Barns were found associated with the camps near the trams or where horses were needed to move material to the flumes. Barns varied greatly in size from 144 to over 3,400 square feet, with half of the barns measuring 500 to 1,500 square feet, or about an average 24x42 foot building.[2] Frequently, the barns were divided into stalls with a hay trough and grain box by each stall (Figures 91–93).

Figure 91 – A typical barn in Crooked John Creek that is in fair condition. 1996. Photograph by B. John Losensky.

Figure 92 – Typical grain box found in most of the barns. 1998. Photograph by B. John Losensky.

Figure 93 – Barn door. 1996. Photograph by B. John Losensky.

At least one camp in the three operations developed into a small community where a store and blacksmith shop, plus the headquarters for the operation, were found. The settlement of McCune or Headquarters was a good example in McCune's operation. Here the workers could buy supplies at the store, and it also provided a voting place during elections.[3] An article in the *Anaconda Recorder* on November 10, 1894, stated that the vote at the camp (McCune) for the new capital was seventy-five votes.[4] McCune maintained a home there, and there was a large blacksmith shop. A sawmill was also located here. Camp Two, or Main Camp, provided similar opportunities in Allen's operation. The Forest Service also maintained an office here where the sale administrator lived. The town of French Gulch also supplied a base for operations, particularly after Nels Pearson took over the operation. A store as well as a sawmill were located here. In Willow Creek there was a camp at both ends of the flume and a small camp in West Fork Willow Creek. No evidence, however, was found that these camps contained stores.

Since lodgepole pine dominated the area, almost all the cabins were built with it. In some cases, they were built from dead trees and even some that had been charred in a fire. Fireplaces were not common and apparently small cast iron stoves were used for heat and cooking (Figure 94).

Figure 94 – Remains of a stove used for heat and cooking. 1996. Photograph by B. John Losensky.

Frequently, the remains of an outdoor rock oven were present for baking bread, particularly where the men were organized and living together (Figures 95–96).

Figure 95 – A company of men gathered around the bread baking oven. 1906. Remains of these ovens were found in all the sale areas. The sign held by the man on the left states "*Questo e il nosteo forno 9 Marzo 1906*" (Italian for "This is our oven, March 9, 1906"). This date was a Friday; it is surprising that they are not working. The photographer's visit may be the reason. Behind the man with the bread is a man holding a snowshoe rabbit. Was this to be supper tonight? PHOTOGRAPH COURTESY OF UNIVERSITY OF MONTANA ARCHIVES AND SPECIAL COLLECTIONS (77-140). PHOTOGRAPHER UNKNOWN.

Figure 96 – Remains of a bake oven found on Allen's sale. 1998. PHOTOGRAPH BY B. JOHN LOSENSKY.

Workers who did the wood hauling usually lived in small settlements. Barns were constructed there in which to stable the horses. These settlements in McCune's or Allen's operations commonly were located near a tram, and the tram crew would live there also. Larger cabins were commonly found here that were used as boarding houses. These frequently had two rooms, with one serving as a kitchen and the other as the room where the workers ate. On occasion a separate cabin provided sleeping quarters. In Camp Two in Allen's operation the boarding house was a two-storied building with sleeping accommodations on the second floor (Figure 75). These larger cabins typically had wooden floors and, commonly, a roof made of boards instead of poles.

During the survey of the three cutting areas, over 230 cabins were located, along with foundations for 40 more.[5] Cabin construction varied to some degree by the year of the logging and the logging operation. An example of how the cabin construction varied was by notch type at the corners. Four types were used in the cabins on Mt Haggin: "U" notch, "V" notch, flat notch, and box corner. The following Tables provide a general idea of the cabin construction based on the cabins that were found.[6]

Table 1 — Percent of Cabins With Various Notch Types by Logging Site

Logging Site	"U" notch	"V" notch	Flat notch	Box corner
McCune	95%	5%	< 1%	0
Willow Creek	82%	11%	4%	4%
Allen	83%	0%	4%	12%

Table 2 — Percent of Cabins by Various Size Classes by Logging Site

Logging Site	<200 sqft	200 – 400 sqft	400+ sqft
McCune	61%	28%	11%
Willow Creek	63%	25%	12%
Allen	51%	37%	12%

"U" Notch

"V" Notch

Flat Notch

Box Corner

Figure 97 – Different styles of corners used on the cabins found in the three sale areas, ca. 1997. PHOTOGRAPHS BY B. JOHN LOSENSKY.

Table 3 — Percent of Cabins by Number of Rooms by Logging Site

Logging Site	1-room	2-room	3-room	4-room
McCune	94%	6%	0	0
Willow Creek	92%	0	4%	4%
Allen	95%	5%	0	0

Of special interest was the lack of dump sites associated with the cabins. While scattered pieces of tin, glass, and other discarded items were common, no concentrated accumulation of cans, which are commonly found in logging camps, were found (Figures 98 & 99). Even in the more permanent camps which contained boarding houses there was an apparant lack of a dump.[7]

Figure 98 – A cast iron pot used for cooking in found in a Willow Creek camp. 1998. Photograph by B. John Losensky.

Figure 99 – Whiskey bottle found by a cabin. Photograph by B. John Losensky.

Other items show how these woodchoppers were able to fashion items to meet their needs where store items were not available (Figures 100–103).

Figure 100 – Cabin door showing handmade closure assembly with lock. 2004. PHOTOGRAPH BY B. JOHN LOSENSKY.

Figure 101 – Saw horse made on site found by one of the cabins. 1999. PHOTOGRAPH BY B. JOHN LOSENSKY.

Figure 102 – Homemade base for a sharpening stone used to sharpen woodworking tools. 2001. PHOTOGRAPH BY B. JOHN LOSENSKY.

Who were these men who labored in the forest? Where did they come from and how did they live in their rough cabins in all kinds of weather, isolated from a permanent community? Were these failed miners who resorted to cutting wood to keep from starving? For some of the immigrants, it may simply have been a job that was available or, in some cases, the former occupation of the person in his home country. Since most wood cutting jobs paid by the cord rather than by the hour, it may have presented an opportunity for a skilled cutter to make more money in the woods than in the mines or the milling operation. Whatever attracted them, working in the woods provided jobs for hundreds of men. Settlement in the Butte area began in the 1860s with the discovery of gold. The 1870 census gives us a first look at the composition of the community. By this time, placer mining was pretty well over, and attempts to mine the silver deposits had limited success. Many of the prospectors had left the area in search of new prospects. Based on the pattern of other mining towns, once the major placer gold was removed the claims were frequently abandoned and an influx of Chinese workers would take up the claims and rework the diggings. By the 1870 census this had occurred in the Butte area, and, consequently, about a third of the approximately 738 men in the area were Chinese. Another third represented US-born men, while the remaining third represented a mixture of foreign countries. Surprisingly, none of them listed their occupation as a wood worker. No doubt this role was filled by men who could not mine during the winter and cut wood to earn enough money to sustain themselves, or each miner obtained his own wood supply. See Table 4 below for a breakdown of the population in 1870.[8]

Table 4 — Country of Origin of Male Residents of Butte Area in 1870. Based on 1870 Census Data

Place of Origin	Silver-Bow Placers	Butte	German Gulch	Total	Percent
China	150	96	5	251	34
US	113	41	84	238	32
Germany	24	7	44	75	10
Ireland	13	14	25	52	7
Canada	18	10	9	37	5
Other	44	16	25	85	12
Total	**362**	**184**	**192**	**738**	100

With the low number of people living in the area and only limited milling operations, demand for wood was probably limited. By 1880, progress had been made in smelting the complex silver ores and mining was rapidly developing. The demand for wood to fire the smelters to process the ores had increased substantially. This demand provided an opportunity for a person to make a living working in the woods, and the 1880 census showed 168 men as woodchoppers and 66 as wood haulers.

Table 5 — Country of Origin of Male Woodchoppers and Wood Haulers in the Butte Area in 1880 Based on 1880 Census Data

Place of Origin	Woodchopper	Percent	Wood Hauler	Percent	Total	Percent
US	98	58	45	68	143	61
Canada	43	26	10	15	53	23
Ireland	7	4	2	3	9	4
England	1	<1	4	6	5	2
Germany	4	2	1	2	5	2
Italy	4	2	0	0	4	2
Other	11	7	4	6	15	6
Total	**168**		**66**		**234**	**100**

While some Chinese were still in the camps in 1880, only one was listed as working in the woods. US- and Canadian-born men dominated this work force, with only 16 percent from other countries. Immigration, however, was increasing as mining activity expanded along with supporting businesses. It was reported in the *New Northwest* that an immigrant train arrived in April 1883, bringing a large number of people to Butte and Deer Lodge.[9] The railroad was transporting emigrants from St. Paul, Minnesota, to any point in Montana for $150 per carload (about $4,427 in 2022 dollars)[10].

The average age of all wood workers in 1880 was almost thirty-two years (Table 6). About 81 percent of the woodchoppers were single, 15 percent married, and the remainder widowed. The proportion of single men seems unusually high, but this may represent the reality of living in the woods on the edge of civilization. The wood haulers, however, were 70 percent single, 24 percent married, and 6 percent widowed. Commonly, the wood haulers lived in small settlements where the horses could be stabled and cared for. These conditions may have been more favorable for a married person rather than living isolated in a lone cabin in the woods.

Table 6 — Average Age and Marital Status of All Wood Workers in 1880 in the Butte Area Based on 1880 Census Data

Place of Origin	Single	Married	Widowed or Divorced	Average of all
US	30	36	45	32
Canada	28	32	45	29
Ireland	41	42		42
England	24	40	53	39
Germany	33	35		34
Italy	35			35
All other	32	30		32
Avg. of all Workers	**30**	**35**	**46**	**32**

Table 7 — Marital Status of Woodchoppers and Wood Haulers in Percent in 1880 in the Butte Area Based on 1880 Census Data

	Single	Married	Widowed or Divorced
Woodchoppers	81	15	4
Wood haulers	70	24	6

In 1885, a document was published listing the residents of Anaconda. A supplemental list was attached which showed the workers living in Caplice and McCune's wood camp near Anaconda. Workers were listed by name and occupation[11] (Table 8 & Appendix D).

Table 8 — List of Number of Employees by Occupation at Caplice & McCune's Camp in 1885–1886

Occupation	Number of Employees	Percent of Employees
Teamster	83	37
Woodchopper	72	32
Laborer	51	23
Clerk	4	2
Cook	4	2
Blacksmith	2	1
Wagon maker	2	1
Freighter	2	1
Bookkeeper	1	<1
Merchant	1	<1
Carpenter	1	<1
Surveyor	1	<1
Total	225	

While the 1880 census listed wood cutters and timber hauler, it did not indicate if any other people in other occupations were associated with the logging industry. Based on the job listings for the camp in Table 8, an additional seventy jobs, or 31 percent, were supported by this operation. These jobs were not accounted for in Table 5 and the total woods jobs in 1880 may have been closer to 300. Since the Caplice and McCune contract was started after the 1880 census, the total number of men working in the woods in 1885 may be closer to 500.

Unfortunately, most of the census information for the year 1890 was destroyed in a fire which occurred in the US Department of Commerce building in Washington, DC, in 1921. The information for the Butte area did not survive the fire. This information would have been significant, as it would have been at the height of McCune's operation when wood was the primary fuel for the camps. Based on stories in the local newspapers, it can be assumed that the number of woods workers in 1890 was probably at least double the number in 1880. This time period probably represented the highest employment for wood workers during the fluming period.

Conversion of the smelters from wood burning to coal burning in 1895 caused a significant drop in wood use. At the same time, however, wood use for other purposes increased as a result of a significant increase in the population by 1900. Consequently, the population of men listed in the 1900 census that worked in the woods was similar to the number in 1880 (Table 9). There was, however, a significant change in the makeup of the work force, with US and Canadian workers dropping to 62 percent and foreign workers increasing to 38 percent. The average age increased to thirty-nine and the proportion of married workers increased significantly to about 23 percent, with 72 percent single and the remainder widowed or divorced (Table 10).

Table 9 — Country of Origin of Males Working in the Woods in the Butte Area in 1900 Based on 1900 Census Data

Place of Origin	Wood Chopper	Percent	Wood Hauler	Percent	Other Wood Jobs	Percent	Total	Percent
US	54	35	21	30	19	50	94	36
Canada	34	22	19	28	14	37	67	26
Italy	20	13	7	10	0	0	27	10
Finland	20	13	5	7	0	0	25	10
Sweden	12	8	5	7	2	5	19	7
Other	15	10	12	17	3	8	30	12
Total	**155**		**69**		**38**		**262**	

Table 10 — Average Age and Marital Status of Wood Workers in the Butte Area Based on 1900 Census Data

Place of Origin	Single	Married	Widowed or Divorced	Average of all
US	36	44	50	38
Canada	36	45	54	40
Italy	36	49	47	39
Finland	39	42	34	40
Sweden	36	29	37	35
All other	38	43	47	40
Avg. of all Workers	**36**	**44**	**49**	**39**

By 1910, the availability of coal and electricity had further impacted the number of wood workers with almost a 50 percent drop in numbers (Table 11). US and Canadian workers also declined to about 36 percent of the work force, with foreign workers increasing to 64 percent. The average age of the workers did not change much from the 1880 census. Married workers increased to about 39 percent of the work force, with 58 percent single (Table 12). Several of the wives of the foreign workers remained in their home country, however.[12]

Table 11 — Country of Origin of Males Working in the Woods in the Butte Area in 1910 Based on the 1910 Census Data

Place of Origin	Wood Chopper	Percent	Wood Hauler	Percent	Other Wood Jobs	Percent	Total	Percent
Italy	33	39	0	0	1	3	34	25
US	13	15	10	56	7	22	30	22
Austria	12	14	0	0	13	41	25	19
Canada	12	14	2	11	5	16	19	14
Finland	7	8	2	11	1	3	10	7
Other	7	8	4	22	5	16	16	12
Total	**84**		**18**		**32**		**134**	

Table 12 – Average Age and Marital Status of Wood Workers in the Butte Area Based on 1910 Census Data

Place of Origin	Single	Married	Widowed or Divorced	Average of all
Italy	30	40		34
US	31	44	59	35
Austria	31	40		36
Canada	46	51		48
Finland	43	35	53	42
All Others	35	47		39
Avg. of all	**34**	**42**	**53**	**38**

Table 13 — List of Number of Employees by Occupation at Allen's Camp in 1910

Occupation	Number of Employees	Percent of Employees
Woodchopper	57	62
Fluming	9	10
Laborer	6	7
Teamster	4	4
Forest ranger	3	3
Forest guard	2	2
Carpenter	2	2
Foreman	2	2
Cook	2	2
Cookhelper	1	1
Merchant	1	1
Stable foreman	1	1
Camp superintendant	1	1
Engineer	1	1
Total	**92**	

The proportion of other occupations in Allen's camp in 1910 was similar to that found in 1885, but with a significant drop in the number of teamsters (Table 13). This drop may indicate the teams were kept in a different camp, as this list includes only the employees in Camp 2. The presence of Forest Service employees also reflects the change in management of the forest reserves (Table 13 and Appendix D).

As mentioned above, most woodcutters were paid by the cord, so a hard worker could probably earn more than those workers paid by the hour. The men working the flume or hauling wood were hourly workers. Information is limited for these workers. In McCune's operation, workers were paid once a year in the fall. During the rest of the year the men were given credit at the company store based on an estimate of how much wood they had cut. Allen's operation also paid by the cord. It is unclear how the men were paid in the Willow Creek operation. The men typically worked a six-day week. After supper the men usually sat around, fixed clothing, read, played cards, or sat and smoked and told stories. A number of camp games such as "rooster fight" or "squirrel" were sometimes played.[13] Sunday was a day of rest or used to do their wash and maintain equipment. However, they never sharpened their axes on Sunday, as it was bad luck and they though they would probably cut their foot the next time they used it. Sunday was also a day to visit friends or, on occasion, get together for singing or playing a mouth organ or fiddle.[14]

One cabin was found with what appeared to be a horseshoe pit, as evidenced by steel pins with horseshoes on them.[15] Parties were held on special days such as the 4th of July or Christmas and people may have come from the surrounding area to join them. One such party on July 29, 1892, at McCune's camp was reported in the *Anaconda Standard*:[16]

> *The ball room was attractively decorated, and the bright lights shown upon the scene of gayety and mirth seldom witnessed in this section. At 9 McCune's camp band struck up the opening music and the grand march followed affording a splendid opportunity for displaying the attractive costumes of the ladies. After the grand march, waltz, quadrille, and polka followed in quick succession until midnight when a delightful banquet was served. At one dancing was resumed and until three ushered in the dawn there was a giddy ceaseless whirl. It was a pleasantest affair ever given at McCune's camp and all who attended went away happy. Among those who participated in the dance were Mrs. King, Miss Hobson of Anaconda, the Misses Jones of Mill Creek, Miss Grome and Mrs. Lindsay of Big Hole, Mr. & Mrs. Parker and daughters, Messrs Neff, Davidson, McCune, Wiles, Geigerich, Claridge, Parker and Lindsay.*

Another story from the *Anaconda Standard* describes the men engaged in snowshoe races:[17] "*They are having a whole lot of fun these days at McCune's camp running or sliding snowshoe races. The Finns are the most expert, though they have found a close competitor in Mr. Dudley who recently made a mile down a steep declivity in 2 minutes and 15 seconds.*" These were actually ski races. The skis were quite long and a long pole was commonly used to propel them and to use as a rudder for steering.

There are also stories of some of the loggers riding logs down the flume to have a little excitement. Young boys were also attracted to this sport, and after spending a day fishing on Mill Creek, they would ride the flume home. Since this activity was frowned on by parents, they would have to wait until their clothes dried before getting home. In 1891, a woodchopper was killed by a falling tree. Because of the isolated spot of the accident, the only way to get the body out was down the flume.[18]

For many of the men the trip to town was probably the high point of their social life. Unfortunately, these trips also led to fights, which were commonly reported in the papers of the day. The *Semi-Weekly Miner* reported that "*a fight or two signalized the opening up of the ceremonies of Christmas day. As they were the result of the peculiarly bracing character of the climate at this elevation combined with beer, and as no bones were broken, nor a display of deadly weapons made no arrests followed. The leading actors in the affrays were adorned with extra heads and the fun went on as though the little interruption had been 'billed' for the occasion.*"[19]

In some cases, workers heading to town could become victims, as indicated in a story in the *Anaconda Standard.*[20] "*A female vampire, whose headquarters are near LaVeta St., was arrested last night by officer McManus for begging money. She is also charged with robbing a woodchopper of several dollars.*" In other cases, the trip may lead to problems in town or when they returned to camp. The *Anaconda Standard* reported that "*Alexander Simpson was arrested early yesterday morning for breaking into George Burke's house. Simpson has been employed at McCune's camp for some time. He had worked at the smelters until they closed down. A couple of days ago he came to town and has been drinking since then.*"[21]

Their "night out" could also follow them back to their job. A news article in the *Anaconda Standard* stated:

> *James Harris worked for Charles Heinze who had a crew who were engaged working on the flume about four miles up the canyon.* [James] *managed to make a good deal of trouble and was told by Heinze to go back from where the men were at work to the camp. Arriving their Harris, wanted cheese which was furnished and then wanted pie. One of the women started to cut a fresh-made pie but he then insisted that he wanted the whole pie. After a time the man's talk became worse than offensive and when Mr. Heinze came in at noon he informed Harris that it would be to his advantage to get out of the camp. Harris objected and in his excited talk he called Heinze an Irishman and that broke Charlie Heinze all up, as it amused everybody who heard of it. When the men came down from the flume at dinner and learned how Harris had conducted himself they quietly escorted him to the edge of the camp and instructed him to leave without any delay. Harris has been on the flume work for some time and is ordinarily a good enough fellow, but yesterday's affair was close after his pay-day.*[22]

In other cases a trip to town could end with tragic results. A story in the *Anaconda Standard* stated that:

> *Nels Pearson, manager of the Willow Creek Fluming company, with headquarters at Willow Creek, a station a few miles east of Anaconda on the B.A. & P. railroad, came to the city last evening and announced to the authorities that he had killed Andrew Hipala, one of the employees of the company. Pearson called upon County Attorney Tolan and briefly told his story. He said that he was in Anaconda yesterday and returned to Willow Creek station on the train leaving this city at 2:46 in the afternoon. Upon his arrival home he was told by his wife that Andrew Hipala was drunk and making threats against his life. Pearson was in the office of the company, and he noticed that Hipala was standing at the door with an axe in his hands. He picked up a short club and, stepping to the door, struck Hipala just above and behind the left ear, crushing in*

> *his skull. In a short time the man died and Coroner Walsh was notified. Pearson told the county attorney that his own life was certainly in danger, and said the man undoubtedly intended to hit him with the axe he had in his hand. He also told the attorney that he had never had any trouble with the man and was at a loss to understand why Hipala should want to take his life. After telling his story to the county attorney, Pearson was turned over to Sheriff Fleming and it is said he was locked up. Hipala was a man about 40 years of age and said to be a native of Sweden. But little is known about him except that he had been employed by the Willow Creek Fluming Company for some time. The only witnesses to the affair say that Hipala was drunk and did not seem to know what he was doing.*[23]

Working in the woods was dangerous work and injuries were common. With work continuing year-round, winter added another risk factor. The *Semi-Weekly Miner* carried a story that highlights the danger of winter logging:

> *With the commencement of the winter wood hauling business and the freezing up of the roads, accidents to wood haulers seem to have become epidemic. During the past ten days the Miner has recorded no less than five serious, and two fatal accidents of this character. Yesterday afternoon as Harry M. Bright was driving a wood team down the Centerville grade; he walked by the side of the load in order to attend to the brake, which was an ordinary chain lock. Thinking the lock was slipping, he attempted to secure the chain without stopping the team, and in stooping over, at the same time walking along with the wagon, his foot came in contact with a frozen rut, and he was thrown headlong under the wheels of the heavily laden wagon. The rear wheel passed over him, breaking his right leg below the knee and crushing his left thigh bone. The unfortunate man was taken up in an unconscious condition and conveyed to the Sisters' Hospital, where his leg was set, and wounds dressed by the hospital physicians.* [24]

Inexperience was also a factor for newly arrived workers, as described in the following article:

> *Monday morning in Elk Park, occurred another one of those distressing accidents which every few weeks break in on the peaceful yet laborious seclusion of the hundreds of sturdy men now making a living by chopping wood on Government lands. A young man named Harvey Ely was working with his uncle, Edward Ely, at a point known as Watering Trough. Young Ely is only twenty-one years of age, and has not been very long in the Territory, having recently come out from Salem, Mo. He was chopping wood, and being a muscular young fellow, was delivering some powerful blows with his ax, when, through someone of the many mysterious incidents which influence human life, the blade of the ax slipped, and entering the right foot at the instep, severed that member almost entirely, leaving it hanging by a slender band of flesh. The pain and loss of blood were of course great, and Edward Ely, the uncle, wrapped his foot at once as well as was possible under the circumstances and at the earliest possible moment brought the wounded man into the Sisters' Hospital. Yesterday amputation was performed by Dr. Hough and Johnston. Our informant met the elder Ely yesterday, returning to his camp where he is hauling for James Talbot and learned from him the above particulars.*[25]

In another case reported by the *Anaconda Standard*, a man was killed in the Twelvemile wood camp in 1893:

> *At about 6 o'clock on the evening of the accident he told his partners, one of whom was his brother-in-law Bigengiari Benvenuto to go to the cabin and prepare supper and that after he fell the tree then nearly chopped down, he would go to a neighbors cabin and get a sack of flour. Though he did not come home that night nothing unusual was thought of the matter as he was in the habit of staying away all night. In the morning, however, his partners became alarmed and when they arrived at the place where they worked the previous day, they found several men there looking at the dead body. It is presumed the unfortunate man had felled the tree upon branches of two adjoining trees, that he did then chop one of them sufficiently to cause all three to fall and was caught by one of them and killed. . . . The deceased was about 45 years of age and leaves a wife and two children who reside in a small chalet near Florence, Italy.*[26]

In some cases an injury led to other problems for the woodchopper, as described by an article in the *Anaconda Standard:*

> *A woodchopper was brought from Mill Creek yesterday terribly cut about the chin and cheek. He was faint from loss of blood, but his wounds are not considered serious. Early last evening the fellow felt comfortable and came downtown by slow stages. But once on Main St. he sought further comfort in frequent doses of liquid lightning with the result he was carried to the hospital at 10 pm a completely ruined fellow. His head was worse than ever, his stomach was in a state of insurrection and he had lost a check and some loose change that he had in his pocket.*[27]

Over the period from May 1882 until December 1914, there were twenty-one reported deaths and twenty-six injuries to wood workers reported in the papers.[28] Falling trees were responsible for four deaths and three injuries. Accidents hauling wood were the cause of two killed and three injured. Seven injuries were reported for axe cuts, and probably only the worst cases made it to the papers. A group of unidentified accidents caused four deaths and three injuries. Fighting resulted in three deaths and four injuries. Generally, alcohol was involved in these arguments. Another death was attributed to alcohol when the person fell into the river during the winter and froze to death. Accidents on the flume or at the "dump" resulted in one death and six injuries. Only two deaths were attributed to a health condition. Finally, there were four deaths as a result of suicide. The *Anaconda Standard* reported on May 30, 1905, on one of these cases in Willow Creek:[29]

> *Gabriel Danielson, a wood-chopper employed by Pearson & Johnson, wood contractors, doing business on Upper Willow Creek killed himself in his lonely cabin three or four days ago. The body was taken in charge yesterday evening by Coroner Walsh and brought to this city. It is hardly probable that an inquest will be held, although it has not yet been definitely decided. It was without any doubt a case of suicide and the reason for it was despondency. Just why the man should be despondent is, however, not so clear. When he was found some money and several hundred dollars in deposit checks were in his pocket. He had plenty of provisions in his cabin and had the ability to earn good money chopping cordwood. He lived alone in his cabin, which is some considerable distance from any other cabin in that neighborhood, but those with whom*

he usually conversed say that he frequently spoke of being tired of life and had a notion to kill himself. These remarks, while frequently made, did not cause his companions to think he actually contemplated anything of the kind. They supposed the man was merely talking as some men do when feeling bad. He was not a heavy drinker; in fact, it is claimed he seldom drank anything stronger than a glass of beer. He was rather too old for a love affair and therefore the suicide is somewhat of a mystery to his companions. Those who know the man say he was a native of Finland and that he was about 50 years of age. He has lived in and around Anaconda for the past 11 or 12 years or perhaps even longer. He was a man of good character and was always very prompt in the payment of his obligations. He was a money maker and saved all he made and in addition to the certificates found on his person, is supposed to have other money or property either in this country or in his native land. Just how much no one seems to know. There are no relatives in this country and the only letters found in the cabin are in the Swedish language. The cabin is situated about six miles up Willow creek from the B.A.&P. station of that name. It is not known when the act was done, but as he was not seen for the past five days by any of the other woodchoppers it is supposed the deed was done three or four days ago. The body was found lying on the bunk with a revolver on the breast; it having evidently fallen from the man's hand after the fatal bullet was fired. A prayer book was found on a small stand near the head of the bed and the conclusion of those who visited the place is that he read the prayer book and then placed the muzzle of the revolver in his mouth and pulled the trigger. The course of the bullet was slightly downward and it lodged in the spine at the base of the brain. From the unmoved position of the body it is surmised that death was instantaneous. There was no struggle after the shot was fired. The cabin was locked on the inside and it was necessary to break it open. Some of the other wood-choppers thought it rather strange that Danielson had not been around for a day or two and two of them went to his cabin yesterday morning. They found the cabin door locked and out of curiosity looked through the little window. It was with horror that they gazed at the lifeless body on the bunk and they lost no time in reporting the matter to the contractors, Pearson & Johnson. A messenger was at once dispatched to town after the coroner and while waiting for that official several men went to the cabin, broke it open and prepared the body for shipment to this city. It is claimed that Danielson has always enjoyed good health and was a strong and robust man. The only way his companions can account for the suicide is that he became lonely and despondent.

As can be gathered from the above events, life in the woods was hard. Serious injury was just a step away and a man's yearly earnings gone with a drop of a match or stroke of lightning. His ability to earn a living became a concern as the woodchopper aged, and depression was not uncommon. A number of the men who immigrated to America had left their wife and family in the old country and were never able to earn enough money to pay for their trip to bring them to America, or were killed before it happened. No government plans were available to help him through periods of sickness or when logging operations were shut down. Consequently, woodchoppers appeared to live for the moment with short bursts of partying and long periods of isolation and hard work. Wood workers lived hard and frequently died young.

CHAPTER EIGHTEEN

Settlement of Past Sins

With the transfer of the forest reserves into the Department of Agriculture in 1905, the General Land Office (GLO) in the Department of Interior undertook a survey of the Butte area to determine conditions at the time of the transfer. Field investigations revealed a serious problem with past management. Large areas of the reserve had been cut over in the Mill Creek, Deep Creek, and Willow Creek drainages with no record of payment or control by the government.[1] Allen had already logged for a year in the California Creek area when the survey was conducted, and his operation was immediately suspended since he did not have a contract for the timber. By subsequently negotiating a timber sale with the Forest Service, he was able to avoid additional penalties other than an obligation to pay for the material he removed and to do the appropriate cleanup of slash left on the ground. The other cuttings were not as easily resolved.

A flurry of activity followed, with a number of cases filed against past logging operators. Nels Pearson was charged with illegal cutting on June 30, 1906, and on July 6, 1906. Two other trespass cases were filed against Richard E. DeKay and Alfred A. McCune by Special Agent A.W. Lafferty from the GLO. In the reports, Lafferty cites Nels Pearson for trespass in Willow Creek as well as DeKay, who also logged in Willow Creek. Alfred McCune was charged with trespass in Mill and Deep Creeks. Lafferty estimated that the government should recover about $15,000 ($496,650 in 2022 dollars) from Pearson, $6,000 ($98,660 in 2022 dollars) from DeKay, and $500,000 ($16,555,000 in 2022 dollars) from McCune.[2] The reports were forwarded to H.H. Schwartz, chief of Fourth Field Division, who found them incomplete and the charges not supported by sufficient evidence to warrant a suit. The result was that no charges were brought at that time.[3]

Forest Supervisor of the Deerlodge National Forest C.C. Hall decided to investigate the McCune area cuttings and made arrangements to have the area surveyed. Louis L. Sharp, who followed H.H. Schwartz as chief of the Fourth Field Division in the Department of Interior, found out about Hall's plan. On January 13, 1908, Sharp wrote to the commissioner of the General Land Office (GLO) stating that based on a letter of September 27, 1907, from the commissioner of GLO, that all cases committed prior to the establishment of a forest reserve were to be handled by the Department of Interior.[4] He indicates that he just recently found out that the Forest Service was going ahead with plans to have the cutting surveyed and mapped. He was concerned that there might be a misunderstanding with the Forest Service, and he wanted them notified of this decision. Mr. Hall may have started this investigation to get some action going on the trespass, as it had been over a year since it had been reported but no action had yet been taken. One of the key issues that would determine the outcome of these cases related to how the land was classified. If it was considered mineral land, then under the mining law of 1878 it was permissible to harvest the timber to support the mining activity.[5] Since a classification of the land had never been conducted, the mining interests assumed that all land was mineral and open to harvest. The Forest Service countered with a claim that there was no proven mineral value on the area that had been cut. Based on a letter dated July 24, 1908, from Chief Sharp to the commissioner of GLO, the Department of Interior finally began a survey of the McCune cuttings.[6] He states that he had a crew in the field conducting a survey of the activity and explained the process they used to determine the volume of timber removed. Edward Doyle and L.S. Ropes were responsible for the survey. A follow-up letter, dated August 22, 1908, described in more detail the survey method and that *"No one can appreciate the immensity of the trespass until he has gone over it—when one figures that there was in the neighborhood of 9,600,000 trees cut and removed from some 60 sections of land, which was manufactured into about 1,000,000 cords of wood valued at about $3,000,000. . . ."* (about $97,170,000 in 2022 dollars)[7].

Doyle filed his report on June 30, 1908, and Ropes filed his on July 6, 1908.[8] The reports indicated that the investigation was begun on June 22 of that year. They made a survey of the area logged south of the Continental Divide and Doyle made the following conclusion: "*There is nothing to be seen or found on this entire area cut over that would offer any inducement to a miner or prospector to spend any time expecting to find any mineral in either quartz or placer. . . . In view of the above facts gathered from this investigation, I am fully satisfied that the land this timber was cut over is strictly non-mineral land.*" In August, Edward Doyle reexamined a portion of the area and investigated the small rock crusher found in Section 3 T3N, R12W near the head of Sevenmile Creek. He also evaluated some digging in upper Twelvemile Creek. Those diggings were outside the area logged and the ore for the crusher was also brought in from outside the cutting area and did not amount to anything. He again stated that none of the area cut could be considered mineral land[9] (Figure 103).

The survey actually only covered all or part of forty-nine sections and showed 12,610 acres cut and 720,683 cords removed.[10] The survey was completed on November 6, 1908, and a report sent to the Commissioner of the GLO with recommendations for legal action on January 15, 1909.[11] There was an immediate follow-up when it was discovered that the structure of the company had changed from a partnership to a corporation. This made it difficult to determine who the suit should list for collection of damages.[12] James Haggin, Marcus Daly, Lloyd Tevis, and George Hearst were all prime candidates. In addition, the Anaconda Mining Company also was responsible, along with the men in charge of the actual cutting—David Neagle and Alfred McCune.[13]

On June 30, 1909, Howard J. Atwell, the lead investigator for the McCune trespass, sent a letter to the commissioner outlining the organizational structure of the Anaconda Company.[14] During 1895, the four principal owners of the old Anaconda Mining Company sold all their property to the new company, Anaconda Copper Mining Company, and subsequently sold a one-fourth interest in the new company to the London Exploration Company (Rothschilds). Atwell comments: "*. . . the above facts present one of the most unique and ingenious plans to hand a foreign corporation a good slice of watered stock; to divide a fabulous amount of wealth, which should be the capital stock of the old Company, the Anaconda Mining Company, among themselves, and to defraud the United Sates Government of nearly $2,000,000 worth of timber belonging to it,*

Figure 103 – Crusher described in the mineral survey found in Sevenmile Creek. 1998. PHOTOGRAPH BY B. JOHN LOSENSKY.

converted to the use of the Anaconda Mining Company." The old company was kept active on account of the contemplated suits by the United States Government for timber trespasses committed by it in the Bitterroot Valley and elsewhere.[15] It was decided, however, to drop the Anaconda Mining Company from the suit, as it had no tangible property after transferring it all to the Anaconda Copper Mining Company in 1895. Tevis was also dropped from further consideration, as he had died and there was no direct information linking him to the logging operation.[16] Frank Hall, special assistant to the attorney general, also recommended that McCune be dropped from consideration, as he was considered financially irresponsible and was mixed up in promoting railroad and mining projects in Peru.[17] Since Neagle logged only a minor area, it was decided to not pursue him in the case either. Mr. Hall recommended that the government should pursue charges against James Haggin and the estates of Marcus Daly and George Hearst.[18]

In the meantime, investigations continued along with interviewing potential witnesses. While the McCune case attracted the most attention, the suits against Nels Pearson and Richard DeKay mentioned in the 1906 letter were also being investigated. On August 30, 1909, Special Agent Luther Hauberg sent a letter to the commissioner concerning the DeKay case.[19] It states, "*One of the witnesses relied upon by Mr. Lafferty to prove his case, Mr. Charles DuBey, is now dead; and the other witness, Mr. I.W. Salisbury, is a drunken, dissolute character who could not be depended upon.*" Hauberg also states that several parties including Pearson had been cutting in the area and it would be impossible to determine what was actually cut by DeKay. DeKay also offered to open his books to the investigation if he was granted immunity and not charged with theft. It was recommended the case be dropped against DeKay and to use him as a witness. Since Pearson was charged for trespass in the same area, his case was also dropped for the same reasons. Pearson also obtained a timber sale which probably covered the area he had already logged plus additional area to continue his operation.[20]

Then, on September 4, 1909, Chief Sharp sent a letter to the commissioner stating they had gotten a statement from Henry Geigerich, who was employed for a number of years by McCune and was involved in the cutting operations. Chief Sharp felt that they had sufficient information to contact the Department of Justice and begin proceedings against the members of the Anaconda Copper Mining Company.[21] The commissioner responded in a letter on November 26, 1909, asking for additional information and also to eliminate some of the area considered in the trespass for various reasons.[22] Whether this was the result of Montana's Congressman Thomas Carter putting pressure on the Interior Department or whether there were actual problems with the case is unclear, but it continued to delay any action against the company. Chief Sharp responded on December 15, 1909, and addressed the concerns of the commissioner.[23] It was determined that the odd sections in T3N, R12W and Section 27 T4N, R11W should be dropped from the suit, as they were railroad sections. In addition, the volume cut from the patented mineral claims in Section 22 T4N R11W was dropped. It was also necessary to drop the lumber cut in the sale area as it was not possible to show who received it. More than likely it was used in the construction of the flume. As a result, the total timber charged against the company was reduced to 562,729 cords with a value of $1,406,722.50 (about $46,070,162 in 2022 dollars) based on the trespass being willful.[24]

No correspondence referencing the case was located for the period between 1910 and 1911. Howard Atwell and others continued to take depositions from people who were employed in the fluming operation or had knowledge of the logging activity. While Frank Hall initially recommended dropping McCune from the suit, the GLO continued to include him in the case. A letter dated July 23, 1912, from Frank Hall to the assistant attorney general discussed his attempt to serve a summons on McCune.[25] He states that McCune could not be found and was in hiding because of some serious difficulty with James Haggin over a mining operation in Peru. His son also killed a man in Peru and he and his son were being sought by some Peruvians who had sworn vengeance against both of them. The son had been put in prison in Peru under sentence of death but escaped and came to Salt Lake, where he injured a woman in a car accident and was now also hiding from local authorities. On November 19, 1912, Frank Hall sent another letter to the attorney general stating that he again attempted to serve the summons on McCune but found he was gone.[26] He decided to give a copy of the complaint to Mrs. McCune on November 4, 1912, but found out they had McCune's first name wrong. They had it listed as Albert rather than Alfred. A revised complaint was finally served on November 6, 1912.[27] At the same time, a complaint was being served on Haggin.[28] A suit was prepared but apparently dropped against George Hearst's estate. Since Hearst, Daly, and Tevis were all dead by this time, it was decided it would be too difficult to sue the estates of these men.[29]

During the period of cutting, it was permissible to remove timber from public lands free of charge if it was considered mineral lands. Consequently, the primary defense of the defendants for their actions was that they cut from mineral lands. As a result, in July 1913, a second, more detailed field investigation looking at the geological structure of the area was conducted by James M. Hill and assisted by F.K. Houston to determine if any of the cutover area could be considered mineral land. The result of this survey again found that the majority of the cutover lands were not mineral lands.[30]

Two cases were developed against McCune and Haggin. Further investigation, however, found that the damages that could be charged were not the value at the mill. Because of their action during cutting—i.e. piling brush and providing fire protection—the courts would consider the trespass as innocent and the market value of $3.50 per cord would not be allowed, but rather the value that the Forest Service would charge—25 cents a cord—would be charged.[31] Consequently, the amount of damages that could be sought dropped from $1,406,722.50 to $179,350 (a drop in value from about $46,070,162 to $5,873,713 in 2022 dollars).[32] An offer of settlement was presented by James Haggin on July 22, 1913, for $100,000 with the stipulation that, by accepting the offer, charges would be dropped against the Hearst estate.[33] After receiving this offer, Frank Hall suggested that the government should seek $179,000 for settlement. However, with the trial expected to be very expensive and the value of the stumpage subject to question, he felt that it would be reasonable to settle for $150,000.[34] Haggin was willing to settle for $150,000 with the following condition: that all complaints against James Haggin, the estate of Marcus Daly (deceased), George Hearst (deceased), Phoebe Hearst, the estate of Lloyd Tevis (deceased), the Anaconda Mining Company, the Anaconda Copper Mining Company, and Alfred McCune be dropped.[35] With this offer the case went back to the government, where the following individuals recommended settlement: Ligon Johnson, special assistant to the attorney general; secretary of the interior through A.A. Jones; first assistant secretary; the attorney general through Mr. Knaebel; and Frank Hall, special assistant to the attorney general. When the compromise came before Assistant Secretary of Treasury Byron R. Newton, the difference between the alleged value of the wood and the amount of the compromise was too great for him, and he replied, "*It would be a mere farce to compromise the matter on the basis proposed.*"[36] Discussions continued among the various branches of government and, finally, the secretary of the Treasury requested the report presented by Mr. Hall. Upon review of the report, the secretary of the Treasury reversed his opinion and approved the settlement on April 15, 1914.[37] A letter dated May 6, 1914, to Bitten & Gray Attorneys at Law accepted the compromise and dismissed the cases against Haggin.[38] For some unknown reason the case against Alfred McCune was not dismissed and was still pending the following year. Finally, a letter from Frank Hall to the attorney general brought the oversight up and charges were dismissed on January 4, 1915.[39]

Thus, after eight years of effort, the Anaconda Company, rather than paying the original estimate of damages of $16,555,000, was basically let off with a slap on the wrist and payment of $150,000. No charges were brought against the company for the damage that had been caused on the ground (Figures 104–106). Other than Allen, the operators were never even charged.

Figure 104 – View north from Continental Divide showing Anaconda-Ralston Road following Mill Creek. 1998. The area shows limited recovery after over a 100 years. Erosion on these sites is extensive. PHOTOGRAPH BY B. JOHN LOSENSKY.

Figure 105 – Stumb on a heavily eroded slope on the north side of the Continental Divide. 1998. Note the soil loss around the stump. PHOTOGRAPH BY B. JOHN LOSENSKY.

Figure 106 – Extensive erosion and limited recovery on the north side of the Continental Divide. 1998. Note the erosion channels on the hills in the background. PHOTOGRAPH BY B. JOHN LOSENSKY.

CHAPTER NINETEEN

Epilogue

Although the lawsuit over timber trespass had been settled, there was still concern about the damage to the national forest by smelter fumes. As a result, the federal government continued to press the Anaconda Copper Mining Company for damages. As early as 1906, studies were conducted to determine if sulfur dioxide released from the smelter was causing the damage to the trees in the Anaconda area.[1] Studies in other parts of the nation indicated that the damage being caused in the Anaconda area were the worst in the nation. In 1909, President Theodore Roosevelt decided to bring suit against the Anaconda Company for damage to trees on the national forest. Rather than going directly to court, Roosevelt decided to meet with the company and see if a solution could be worked out.[2] Negotiations continued for years with additional studies conducted to strengthen the government's claims. Finally, in 1910, a lawsuit was filed in the US Circuit Court in Helena, Montana.[3] A year later, a temporary agreement was reached between the company and the government which set up a board to look for solutions to the problem. The company would use the findings of the board to reduce or eliminate the contamination.[4] Litigation dragged on for years with little progress made. During this period, the company bought up much of the private land being impacted by the fumes to reduce the number of suits that could be brought against them. Finally, a bill was passed in Congress in 1922 which expanded the ability of the government to trade national forest lands for private land of equal value.[5] This law provided an option for both parties to solve the issue. By trading away the damaged land for undamaged forested land, the Forest Service would eliminate a serious management problem. The company, on the other hand, would no longer have the federal government trying to control smelter fumes. A total of six separate exchanges took place, with the last one completed in 1937. Lands owned by the company associated with the Lolo, Bitterroot, and other national forests were traded to the Forest Service in exchange for damaged lands around Anaconda. The suit, however, was never settled, and in 1933 the case was marked "Abandoned."[6]

The law to exchange land required the land to have equal value, but unfortunately the damaged land had little merchantable volume remaining. Consequently, to gain equal value, the company was allowed to log portions of the the land they were exchanging. The company was only required to leave 500 to 1,000 board feet per acre and the Forest Service had no control on methods used to log the area. Typically, the trees left were of poor form and condition. Following the trade, the Forest Service had to undertake a recovery plan to mitigate the damage caused by the logging. A prime example of this operation occurred in Rye Creek of the Bitterroot National Forest. Here tractor skidding had been conducted down stream courses, causing significant watershed damage. Some streams had to be entirely rebuilt and others required extensive erosion control measures. Many acres were also planted and some of the remaining timber was removed, as it was high risk to mortality. Roads built to do the original logging encroached into the streams. Work to stabilize them was still occurring into the late 1990s.[7]

The settlement included all the area north of the Continental Divide and the majority of land south of the divide that had been damaged. For some reason, this included areas in the American Creek drainage that apparently suffered little damage. The remaining areas south of the Continental Divide that had limited smelter damage continued to be part of the Deerlodge National Forest and the upper portion of Willow Creek became part of the Beaverhead National Forest.

The traded lands were held by the Anaconda Company until 1965 when the Mount Haggin Livestock Company acquired title to a major portion of the land. They had been leasing the land from the company for their sheep operation based out of the Mule Ranch.[8] In 1976, the Nature Conservancy (TNC) purchased the land from the Mount Haggin Livestock Company and held it in trust until Montana Fish, Wildlife, and Parks and the Forest Service could gather funds to purchase the property from TNC. The land was purchased with Land and Water Conservation Fund (LWCF) and state hunter license dollars, with some of the land added to the Deerlodge National Forest and the remaining area becoming the Mount Haggin State Wildlife Management Area. When the state and federal government acquired the land, there was an active timber sale on the area covered by a ten-year contract with Lousiana Pacific Corporation. Most of the sale was confined to the area in the Willow Creek drainage and Allen's old sale area. Logging continued into the mid 1980s.[9]

And so ended an epic period in the history of logging for the Anaconda Company. Today the hills are quiet with the departure of the hundreds of men who labored here to make a living. The area now provides recreation for hunters, skiers, and people just out for a walk or drive in a forest environment, as well as being a great place for various wildlife species to fulfill their role in the cycle of life of our forests.

Notes

Chapter One
Development of Mining in the Butte Area

1. The public domain was land acquired from foreign governments or by treaty with Native American groups and owned by the federal government. It did not include those lands set aside as reservations for the Indian Nations or given to the states as school trust lands.

2. Marsh, George D., *Copper Camp*, 1970, 1943. The discovery of gold on Butte Hill was made in July 1864 by G.O. Humphrey and William Allison, p. 14.

3. Ibid., p. 16.; Malone, Michael P., *The Battle for Butte,* 1981, pp. 9–10.

4. Taylor, Bill & Jan, *The Butte Short Line*, 1998, p. 7.

5. Marsh, George D., *Copper Camp*, 1970, 1943, pp. 16–17. Malone, Michael P., *The Battle for Butte,* 1981, pp. 9–10.

6. US Department of the Interior, Office of the Census, Ninth Census of the United States, 1870.

7. Marsh, George D., *Copper Camp*, 1970, 1943, p. 296.; Ibid., pp. 11–12; *The Iowaville Roster,* September 19, 2008.

8. US Department of the Interior, Office of the Census, Tenth Census of the United States, 1880.

9. Malone, Michael P., *The Battle for Butte,* 1981, pp. 11–12.

10. Ibid., pp. 15–18.

11. Ibid., pp. 18–19.

12. Glasscock, C.B., *The War of the Copper Kings,* 1962, 1935, p. 70.

13. George Hearst was born near Sullivan, Missouri, on September 3, 1820. He worked on the family farm and eventually improved the farm's profitability so that he could open a small store and lease a couple of lead mines. In 1850, using the money he made from his mining operation, he moved his family to California and found a good gold-bearing quartz ledge which he successfully developed. When he heard of the silver strikes in Nevada, he sold his mine and bought a one-sixth interest in the Ophir Mine. This mine was also very successful. During this period, he and Marcus Daly became friends. https://everipedia.org/Ontario_silver_mine.

14. US Inflation calculator: 1635–2022, Department of Labor data: https://www.in2013dollars.com.

15. Malone, Michael P., *The Battle for Butte,* 1981, pp. 19–27.

16. Taylor, Bill & Jan, *The Butte Short Line*, 1998, p. 7.

17. Malone, Michael P., *The Battle for Butte,* 1981, pp. 27–29.

Chapter Two
Early Logging and Transportation History

1. Malone, Michael P., *The Battle for Butte,* 1981, p. 8.

2. Forest products used in the mining operation included lagging which consisted of planks or timber used to prevent rocks from falling in a mine shaft; stulls which were timbers used to support the roof of the mine shaft; and converter poles that were used in the smelting process. Green converter poles were added to the molten copper to reduce the oxides in the copper. Panskin, A.J. et al., 1950. Forest Products McGraw-Hill Book Company, New York, p. 85; Oudiz, J.J. December 1973. Poling processes for copper refining, Journal of Metals., pp. 35–38.

3. US Department of the Interior, Office of the Census, Ninth Census of the United States, 1870.

4. Malone, Michael P., *The Battle for Butte,* 1981, p. 10.

5. Ibid., pp. 10–16.

6. *Semi-Weekly Miner*, December 5, 1876.

7. Ibid., February 13, 1877.

8. Ibid., March 27, 1877.

9. Ibid., July 10, 1877

10. Ibid., July 10, 1877.

11. Ibid., December 18, 1877. See Chapter 4 for additional discussion on this subject.

12. Ibid.

13. Ibid., April 30, 1878.

14. US Department of the Interior, Office of the Census, Tenth Census of the United States, 1880.

15. *Semi-Weekly Miner*, July 24, 1879; December 14, 1880; US Inflation calculator: 1635–2022, Department of Labor data: https://www.in2013dollars.com.

16. Se*mi-Weekly Miner,* February 8, 1882.

17. Ibid., July 11, 1882; November 15, 1882; US Inflation calculator: 1635–2022, Department of Labor data: https://www.in2013dollars.com.

18. Ibid., August 5, 1882.

19. *New Northwest*, December 14, 1883.

20. A team of horses could pull a wagon about 1.5 times heavier than their weight during a regular workday, which represents about 5,100 pounds. A cord of mixed green and dry lodgepole pine weights about 34 pounds per cubic foot and there are about 95 cubic feet in a cord of wood, or 3,230 pounds per cord. A two-cord load of wood therefore would weigh about 6,460 pounds and be a heavy load. https://www.horseforum.com; Forestry Handbook 1956, pp. 14–30, 1–48.

Chapter Three
Flumes Arrive in Butte

1. Angel, Myron, ed., *History of Nevada: With Illustrations and Biographical Sketches of its Prominent Men and Pioneers, 1881*, pp. 188–191.

2. Ibid., p. 191.

3. US Inflation calculator: 1635–2022, Department of Labor data: https://www.in2013dollars.com.

4. Angel, Myron, ed., *History of Nevada: With Illustrations and Biographical Sketches of its Prominent Men and Pioneers, 1881*, p. 190.

5. *Semi-Weekly Miner*, October 14, 1879.

6. Ibid., September 23, 1882.

7. Ibid., April 11, 1883.

8. US Inflation calculator: 1635–2022, Department of Labor data: https://www.in2013dollars.com.

9. *Semi-Weekly Miner*, July 4, 1883.

10. *Helena Daily Independent*, August 20, 1883.

11. *Semi-Weekly Miner*, October 10, 1883.

12. *New Northwest*, May 25, 1883.

13. US Inflation calculator: 1635–2022, Department of Labor data: https://www.in2013dollars.com.

14. *New Northwest*, October 19, 1883 & October 26, 1883.

15. Ibid., July 11, 1884, & August 23, 1884.

16. *Weekly Anaconda Review*, September 30, 1886; US Inflation calculator: 1635-2022, Department of Labor data: https://www.in2013dollars.com.

17. *Semi-Weekly Miner*, September 23, 1882 & September 30, 1882.

18. *New Northwest*, May 15, 1885; *Semi-Weekly Miner*, April 13, 1887.

19. US Inflation calculator: 1635–2022, Department of Labor data: https://www.in2013dollars.com.

20. *Weekly Anaconda Review*, October 14, 1886.

21. *Semi-Weekly Miner*, April 13, 1887.

22. Ibid., January 12, 1887.

23. Ibid., December 22, 1886.

24. Ibid., September 24, 1887.

25. *Anaconda Standard*, August 12, 1895.

Chapter Four
Public Land and Timber Cutting

1. Gordon, Greg, *When Money Grew on Trees*, 2012. See Chapters 6 and 7 for a discussion of issues in the public domain.

2. *Semi-Weekly Miner*, January 22, 1878.

3. Ibid., April 30, 1878.

4. Ibid., May 31, 1882.

5. Deposition by W.A. Taylor in the case P-45899, p. 149, National Archives. Taylor stated: *"that he and four other men were each given a thousand dollars by a man, whose name he refused to mention, interested in the wood cutting operations in question and told by him to lose said money to a Government Official, whose name he did not remember, then making an investigation of said cutting operations, in a poker game; that he and the other men followed instructions."*

6. *Semi-Weekly Miner*, December 27, 1881.

7. Ibid., February 8, 1882.

8. Ibid., October 25, 1882.

9. *New Northwest*, July 6, 1883.

10. Maps of Montana, https://www.oldmapsonline.org/map/rumsey/2134.05.

Chapter Five
Early History of the Anaconda Company

1. *New Northwest*, May 18, 1883.

2. *Semi-Weekly Miner*, February 28, 1883.

3. *New Northwest*, February 16, 1883.

4. Ibid., May 18, 1883.

5. Ibid.

6. US Inflation calculator: 1635–2022, Department of Labor data: https://www.in2013dollars.com.

7. *New Northwest*, May 18, 1883.

8. *Weekly Anaconda Review*, January 13, 1887.

9. *New Northwest*, May 18, 1883. US Inflation calculator: 1635–2022, Department of Labor data: https://www.in2013dollars.com.

10. Ibid., March 2, 1883.

11. Ibid., June 22, 1883.

12. Ibid., July 6, 1883.

13. *Semi-Weekly Miner*, July 14, 1883. US Inflation calculator: 1635–2022, Department of Labor data: https://www.in2013dollars.com.

14. Butte Court Records, Book I, pp. 157–161.

15. *New Northwest*, August 3, 1883.

16. Ibid., August 17, 1883.

17. Ibid., August 3, 1883.

18. Ibid., October 12, 1883.

19. Ibid., March 14, 1884.

20. Ibid., April 18, 1884.

21. Ibid., September 12, 1884. US Inflation calculator: 1635–2022, Department of Labor data: https://www.in2013dollars.com.

Chapter Six
The First Timber Contract

1. Taylor, Bill & Jan., *Rails to Gold and Silver*, 1999, pp. 11–12.

2. Wikipedia contributors. "David Neagle." *Wikipedia, The Free Encyclopedia*, https://en.wikipedia.org/w/index.php?title=David_Neagle&oldid=953072733 (accessed May 28, 2020). See also *Encyclopedia of Western Lawman & Outlaws*, 1989. Jay Robert Nash, Da Capo Press, pp. 241, 341: *The Spell of the West – Lawman of the Old West*, https://www.legendsofamerica.com/old-west-lawmen: David Neagle.

3. *The Anaconda Standard*, August 8, 1896.

4. Wikipedia contributors. "David Neagle." *Wikipedia, The Free Encyclopedia*, https://en.wikipedia.org/w/index.php?title=David_Neagle&oldid=953072733 (accessed May 28, 2020).

5. Deposition by John Hay in the case P-45899, p. 158, Record Group 60, Department of Justice, National Archives.

6. Deposition by David Neagle in case P-45899, File 2002.003.346, p. 255, National Museum of Forest Service History; *Anaconda Standard*, August 9, 1896.

7. Deposition by Eli Natha in case P-45899, p. 136 and deposition by Z. Geovanelli p. 137, Record Group 60, Department of Justice, National Archives.

8. *New Northwest*, March 7 & 8, 1884; May 1, 8, 15, 1885; December 11, 1885; *Anaconda Standard*, August 9, 1896.

9. Case file for P-45899, p. 37, Record Group 60, Department of Justice, National Archives.

10. Deposition by David Neagle in case P-45899, File 2002.003.346, p. 255, National Museum of Forest Service History.

11. *Arizona Daily Star*, August 21, 1884.

12. *Oakland Tribune*, November 28, 1925. See also *The Justice and the Lady* by Robert Kroninger for a detailed account of the story leading up to the shooting of state judge David S. Terry by David Neagle, from the Yearbook 1977, of the Supreme Court Historical Society.

Chapter Seven
Daly's Quandary

1. *Helena Daily Independent*, October 28, 1884.

2. *Semi-Weekly Miner*, December 3, 1884.

3. Ibid., December 24, 1884.

4. Montana Historical Society, MC169 (file no. 276). MC169 contains additional background information on the operation of the Anaconda Fluming Company and the Mines Timber Company. Helena, Montana.

5. *Semi-Weekly Miner*, December 24, 1884.

6. Bowen, A. W. & Co., *Progressive Men of the State of Montana*, 1902, p. 352; Miller, Joaquin, *An Illustrated History of the State of Montana*, 1894, pp. 784–785. See also John Caplice, by Major Martin Maginnis: In Contributions to the Historical Society of Montana, Vol. VI, 1907, pp. 451–468.

7. *Missoulian*, July 6, July 27, 1872; *New Northwest*, October 12, 1872.

8. Ibid., May 21, 1874.

9. Bowen, A.W. & Co., *Progressive Men of the State of Montana*, 1902, p. 353.

10. *Semi-Weekly Miner*, March 28, 1883.

11. Whitney, Orson Ferguson, *History of Utah.* March 1892. https://en.wikipedia.org/w/index.php?title=Alfred_W._McCune.

12. *New Northwest*, November 16, 1883.

13. Ibid., December 1, 1883.

14. *Helena Daily Independent*, April 19, 1884.

15. *New Northwest*, February 27, 1884.

16. *Semi-Weekly Miner*, December 24, 1884.

17. *New Northwest*, January 1, 1885.

18. *Semi-Weekly Miner*, July 4, 1885; US Inflation calculator: 1635–2022, Department of Labor data: https://www.in2013dollars.com.

19. Ibid., January 10, 1885.

20. Ibid., March 4, 1885.

Chapter Eight
Early Operations of Caplice and McCune

1. Deer Lodge County records in the case P-45899, pp. 159–160, Record Group 60, Department of Justice, National Archives.

2. Deposition by John Hay in the case P-45899, p. 158, Record Group 60, Department of Justice, National Archives; *Anaconda Standard*, August 9, 1896.

3. Deposition by J.A. Gibson in the case P-45899, pp. 143–144, Record Group 60, Department of Justice, National Archives.

4. Maps developed by Vogel for Anaconda Copper Mining Co. showing vegetative conditions ca. 1912 for the upper Deer Lodge Valley. Land Department Volumes, Anaconda-Deer Lodge Historical Society, Anaconda, MT. Frank Vogel worked for the Forest Service on the Pike National Forest at Bear Creek. He also started the timber survey work on the Coconino National Forest. He had an excellent reputation as a timber cruiser and was employed by the Forest Service to teach his method to Forest Service personnel. He was an outstanding man in his line, but "pretty harsh with his crew." He resigned

around October 1, 1908. After resigning from the Forest Service, he was employed for a period of time surveying lands for the Anaconda Company. According to J.A. Fitzwater's memoir, "Vogel... [was] a hard taskmaster but an excellent teacher." *Early Days of the Forest Service, Vol. 1*, p. 63.

5. Bruce, Eugene, June 4, 1914, *Flumes & fluming*, Bulletin of the United States Department of Agriculture No. 87, p. 36.

6. Kramer, E.W., *Report to District Forester on data obtained on the Allen flume near Anaconda, Montana, and on the Rochet flume near St. Joe, Idaho;* August 21, 1912, p. 32; Personal observation.

7. *New Northwest*, September 25, 1885.

8. Deposition by Henry Geigerich in case P-45899, File 2002.003.353-354, pp. 18, 45, 93. National Museum of Forest Service History; *Anaconda Standard*, January 12, 1913.

9. *Semi-Weekly Miner*, March 11 & 18, 1885; *New Northwest*, March 20, 1885.

10. *New Northwest*, September 25, 1885.

11. Statement of wood received from Caplice & McCune and Anaconda Fluming Co., MC-169-52-19, Montana Historical Society; *Daily Butte Miner*, January 1, 1888.

12. *Weekly Anaconda Review*, May 10, 1884.

13. *Semi-Weekly Miner*, June 24, 1885.

14. *New Northwest*, December 11, 1885.

15. Ibid., April 3, 1885.

16. Ibid., April 17, 1885.

17. Deposition by Henry Geigerich in case P-45899, File 2002.003.346, p. 16, National Museum of Forest Service History.

18. Deposition by Henry Brundy in the case P-45899, p. 132, Record Group 60, Department of Justice, National Archives.

19. Personal observation.

20. Deposition by J.A. Gibson in the case P-45899, pp. 143–144, Record Group 60, Department of Justice, National Archives; Deposition of J. L. Jenkins in the case P-45899, p. 190, File 2002.3.346 National Museum of Forest Service History; *Semi-Weekly Miner*, May 21, 1887.

21. Depositions of J.A. Gibson in the case P-45899, page 189, Record Group 60, Department of Justice, National Archives.; J. L. Jenkins, p. 190, and Edward Doyle p. 298, File 2002.3.346 National Museum of Forest Service History.

22. Ibid.

23. Statement of wood received from Caplice & McCune and Anaconda Fluming Co., MC-169-52-19, Montana Historical Society.

24. *Semi-Weekly Miner*, August 18, 1886.

25. *Weekly Anaconda Review*, September 30, 1886.

26. Memorandum prepared by Frank Hall for the Attorney General, no date, Record Group 60, Department of Justice, National Archives.

27. *New Northwest*, October 16, 1885.

28. See note 4 in Chapter 4.

Chapter Nine
Caplice and McCune Work Camps

1. Maps developed by Vogel for Anaconda Copper Mining Co. showing vegetative conditions ca. 1912 for the upper Deer Lodge Valley, Land Department Volumes, Anaconda-Deer Lodge Historical Society, Anaconda, MT.

2. *The Butte Daily Miner*, January 1, 1889.

3. Maps developed by Vogel for Anaconda Copper Mining Co. showing vegetative conditions ca. 1912 for the upper Deer Lodge Valley, Land Department Volumes, Anaconda-Deer Lodge Historical Society, Anaconda, MT.

4. Deer Lodge County History Group. *In (Under) the Shadow of Mount Haggin*, 1975, p. 50.

5. Deposition by Henry Geigerich in case P-45899, File 2002.003.353-354, p. 8, National Museum of Forest Service History.

6. Ibid, p. 28.

7. *Butte Daily Miner*, January 1, 1899.

8. *Semi-Weekly Miner,* May 21, 1887.

9. Deposition by Henry Geigerich in case P-45899, File 2002.003.353-354, p. 90, National Museum of Forest Service History.

10. Maps developed by Vogel for Anaconda Copper Mining Co. showing vegetative conditions ca. 1912 for the upper Deer Lodge Valley, Land Department Volumes, Anaconda-Deer Lodge Historical Society, Anaconda, MT.

11. Ibid.

Chapter Ten
Ousting Caplice

1. Gordon, Greg, *When Money Grew on Trees*, 2014. See Chapter 8 for a discussion of the political background for ousting John Caplice.

2. Ibid. See Chapter 7 for a discussion of William Andrew Jackson Sparks.

3. Malone, Michael P., *The Battle for Butte*, 1981, pp. 86–87.

4. Ibid., pp. 85–87; Marsh, George D., *Copper Camp*, 1970, 1943, p. 34; Marcosson, Isaac F, *Anaconda*, 1957, pp. 85–86; Bowen, A.W. & Co., *Progressive Men of the State of Montana*, 1902, p. 353. Gordon, Greg, *When Money Grew on Trees*, 2014, pp. 119–165. See these sources for a more detailed discussion of the election.

5. *Semi-Weekly Miner*, March 5, 1887.

6. Ibid., April 6, 1887.

7. Deer Lodge County records in the case P-45899, p. 164, Record Group 60, Department of Justice, National Archives.

Chapter Eleven
The Last Gasp

1. *Semi-Weekly Miner,* May 21, 1887.

2. *Weekly Anaconda Review,* January 13, 1887.

3. Ibid.

4. *Semi-Weekly Miner*, May 21, 1887.

5. *Butte Daily Post,* August 29, 1887. The ad contained the following enticements: "Good timber and good prices, Mill Creek Canyon… Anaconda Fluming Co."

6. *Semi-Weekly Miner*, July 30, 1887.

7. Ibid., December 19, 1888.

8. *Butte Miner*, May 1, 1888: "*Proposals wanted - Proposals will be received up to the 10th of May 1888, at Anaconda, M.T. for the construction of 5 miles of V shaped wood flume. Profile and plans can be seen at Hoge, Daly & Co's Bank, Anaconda after May 1st. For particulars apply to or address Anaconda Fluming Co.*"

9. *Semi-Weekly Miner*, January 16, 1889; *Missoula Gazette*, January 23, 1889.

10. *Anaconda Standard*, February 12, 1893, September 12, 1893, and October 8, 1893.

11. Ibid., December 10, 1893.

12. Ibid., September 5, 1899.

13. The *Butte Daily Post*, April 26, 1889.

14. *Semi-Weekly Miner*, August 10, 21, 28, 31, 1889; *Helena Daily Independent*, August 24, 1889.

15. Ibid., August 31, 1889; August 24, 1889.

16. Deposition by Henry Geigerich in case P-45899, File 2002.003.346, pp. 212–214, National Museum of Forest Service History; *Butte Miner*, January 18, 1891.

17. *Anaconda Standard*, October 4, 1891.

18. Memorandum prepared by Frank Hall for the Attorney General, no date, Record Group 60, Department of Justice, National Archives.

19. *Anaconda Standard*, August 12, 1892.

20. Ibid., August 18 & 20, 1892.

21. Ibid., October 23, 1892.

22. Deposition by Henry Geigerich in case P-45899, File 2002.003.346, p. 94, National Museum of Forest Service History; *Butte Miner*, June 7, 1893.

23. *Anaconda Standard*, April 5, 1895.

24. *Semi-Weekly Miner*, January 16,1884.

25. Ibid.

26. Ibid, January 15, 1887.

27. Ibid., February 2, 1887.

28. Ibid., November 27, 1889.

29. Ibid., December 19, 1888.

30. *Anaconda Standard*, June 8, 1890.

31. Ibid., January 1, 1895.

32. Ibid., November 11, 1895.

33. Letter from J. McGregor to W. Flanagan dated October 19, 1895, MC-196-5-13, Montana Historical Society.

34. Statement from the Anaconda Fluming Company to the Anaconda Mining Company covering the period from December 1894 to April 1895, MC – 169-52-19, Montana Historical Society; Inflation calculator: 1635–2022, Department of Labor data: https://www.in2013dollars.com.

35. *Anaconda Recorder*, October 5, 1895.

36. *Anaconda Standard*, Between November 15, 1895, and April 5, 1897, there were at least seven cases brought against various wood cutting groups in the area.

Chapter Twelve
Other Operations

1. Thomas, Bill & Marilyn, *Elliston: Days Gone By,* 1997, pp. 13–14.

2. *The Anaconda Standard,* December 15, 1894.

3. Deposition by Charles DuBey in case P-45899, pp. 42–44, Record Group 60, Department of Justice, National Archives.

4. *The Anaconda Standard,* February 8, 1896.

5. *New Northwest,* March 6, 1896.

6. *The Anaconda Standard,* April 7, 1898.

7. Ibid., June 23, 1898.

8. *Daily Inter-mountain,* January 20, 1900.

9. Ibid., June 26, 1900.

10. Ibid., December 2, 1901; US Inflation calculator: 1635–2022, Department of Labor data: https://www.in2013dollars.com.

11. *The Anaconda Standard,* June 22, 1901; November 18, 1901.

12. Inflation calculator: 1635–2022, Department of Labor data: https://www.in2013dollars.com.

13. *Daily Inter-mountain*, March 6, 1902.

14. Ibid.

15. Deposition by Charles DuBey in case P-45899, p. 42, Record Group 60, Department of Justice, National Archives.

16. US Department of the Interior, Office of the Census, Thirteen Census of the United States, 1880.

17. Deposition by Charles DuBey in case P-45899, p. 42, Record Group 60, Department of Justice, National Archives.

18. Howard, A.G., *The Saga of Nels Pearson – Montana's Paul Bunyan*; Granite County Museum;

Deer Lodge County History Group, 1975. In (Under) the Shadow of Mount Haggin: The Story of Anaconda and Deer Lodge County from 1863 to 1976. In: pp. 49–53; *Nels Pearson 1867–1936*, (no author). Granite County Museum, Phillipsburg, MT.

19. Maps developed by Vogel for Anaconda Copper Mining Co. showing vegetative conditions ca. 1912 for the upper Deer Lodge Valley, Land Department Volumes, Anaconda-Deer Lodge Historical Society, Anaconda, MT.

20. Butte, Anaconda & Pacific Railway, Records, Maps, Butte-Silver Bow Public Archives, Butte, Montana; Personal observation.

21. Personal observation.

22. Deposition by Charles DuBey in case P-45899, p. 43, Record Group 60, Department of Justice, National Archives.

23. Ibid., pp. 42–43.

24. Letter from Luther T. Hauberg to the Commissioner, General Land Office dated August 30, 1909, in case P-45899, pp. 42–44, Record Group 60, Department of Justice, National Archives.

25. Wikipedia contributors. "Big Hole National Forest." *Wikipedia, The Free Encyclopedia,* https://en.wikipedia.org (accessed January 14, 2022).

26. Record of timber sales on the Deerlodge National Forest from 1906, Deerlodge National Forest.

Chapter Thirteen
A New Player

1. Pinchot, Gifford, *Breaking New Ground*, 1947, pp. 1–108.

2. Bowen, A.W. & Co., *Progressive Men of the State of Montana*, 1902, p. 1628.

3. Kramer, E.W., *Report to District Forester on data obtained on the Allen Flume near Anaconda, Montana and on the Rochet Flume near St. Joe, Idaho*, August 21, 1912, p. 2.

4. Ibid., p. 21.

5. Mason, D.T., *Utilization and Management of Lodge Pole Pine in the Rocky Mountains*, Bulletin of the US Department of Agriculture, Washington, D.C., July 12, 1915, pp. 13–14; US Inflation calculator: 1635–2022, Department of Labor data: https://www.in2013dollars.com.

6. Patten, J.M., Map of the Allen Co. timber sale of 9/12/06, Deerlodge Nat'al Forest.

7. Ibid.

8. Ibid.

9. Ibid.

10 *Anaconda Standard*, December 18, 1910.

11. Kramer, E.W., *Report to District Forester on data obtained on the Allen Flume near Anaconda, Montana and on the Rochet Flume near St. Joe, Idaho*, August 21, 1912, p. 5.

12. Ibid., pp. 5 & 6.

13. *Anaconda Standard*, December 14, 1913.

14. ———, Map of French Gulch logging operation 1905–1912. This map also shows the flumes, trams, roads, and camps plus the cutting method used and the vegetation cover type; Personal observation.

15. Kramer, E.W., *Report to District Forester on data obtained on the Allen Flume near Anaconda, Montana and on the Rochet Flume near St. Joe, Idaho*, August 21, 1912, p. 3.

16. Patten, J.M., Map of the Allen Co. timber sale 9/12/06, Deerlodge Nat'al Forest. This map shows the flumes, trams, and camps plus showing areas of cutting by year between 1906 and 1910.

Chapter Fourteen
Allen's Work Camps

1. Personal observation. The number of buildings is based on what is present today. It is highly likely that there were a number more that have disappeared over time. The use of the cabin was determined by door size and mangers for a barn and size and layout for a boarding house.

2. Patten, J.M., Map of the Allen Co. timber sale of 9/12/06, Deerlodge Nat'al Forest.

3. *Anaconda Standard*, December 14, 1913.

4. Gilluly, Jack, "Haggin's Cross-Country Snowbirds Serve up Local History Fare," *Montana Magazine*, December 1991. (Draft)

Chapter Fifteen
Allen's Troubles

1. Letter from Forest Supervisor E.A. Sherman to the Forester, Washington, DC, dated June 11, 1906, Montana State Archives (Montana State Hospital—Warm Springs).

2. Ibid.

3. When formed the name for the Forest was shown as one word though the town and county continued to use the name Deer Lodge.

4. Letter from Forest Supervisor E.A. Sherman to the Forester, Washington, DC, dated June 11, 1906, Montana State Archives (Montana State Hospital—Warm Springs).

5. Ibid.

6. Timber sale between Allen Gold Mining Company and the Hell Gate Forest Reserve dated July 19, 1906, Montana State Archives (Montana State Hospital—Warm Springs).

7. Ibid.

8. Agreement between the Allen Gold Mining Company and North West Coal Company dated August 27, 1906, Montana State Archives (Montana State Hospital—Warm Springs).

9. *Anaconda Standard*, October 5, 1906.

10. Letter from Allen Company to the Forester, Washington, DC, dated October 21, 1908; Letter from Allen Company to District Forester Missoula, Montana, dated January 28, 1909, Montana State Archives (Montana State Hospital—Warm Springs).

11. Three Special Privilege agreements were initiated between the Allen Company and the Hell Gate Forest Reserve: 1. To operate a wood flume dated January 28, 1908; 2. An agreement to operate a telephone line within the Hell Gate National Forest dated January 28, 1908; and 3. An agreement to construct and maintain a pasture of 640 acres dated April 12, 1908, Montana State Archives (Montana State Hospital—Warm Springs).

12. Personal observation.

13. Letter from Allen Company to the Forester, Washington, DC, dated October 21, 1908, Montana State Archives (Montana State Hospital—Warm Springs).

14. Information on these negotiations can be found in the following documents: 1. Statement of Assets and Liabilities dated September 1, 1908; 2. Letter dated September 17, 1908, addressed to the Board of Directors of the Allen Company; 3. Letter dated October 1, 1908, to S.E. Bliss from J.A. Dunlap, Montana State Archives (Montana State Hospital—Warm Springs).

15. Letter dated December 4, 1908, from Samuel Cross to the Forester (Chief of Forest Service), Washington, DC. Attached is a rebuttal letter from C.C. Hall Forest Supervisor to the District Forester, Washington, DC. Two cover letters are included from W.B. Greeley to the Forester (Chief of Forest Service) dated December 18, 1908, and a letter from the Assistant Forester to W.B. Greeley dated December 23, 1908, acknowledging the report, Record Group 95, National Archives.

16. Gilluly, Jack, "Haggin's Cross-Country Snowbirds Serve up Local History Fare," *Montana Magazine,* December 1991. (Draft)

17. Letter from the Allen Company to District Forester, Missoula, MT, dated January 28, 1909. This extension included seven special conditions. Of interest was a requirement for payments to be made with various amounts due on certain dates. Allen was also required to keep enough timber at the dump to cover the value of the outstanding claims. Lastly, no cutting was allowed after May 1, 1909, until all back payments due were paid, Montana State Archives (Montana State Hospital—Warm Springs).

18. *Anaconda Standard*, November 8, 1909. People in attendance were Lieut. Gov. & Mrs. W.R. Allen, G.E. Voyer, & J.C. Harrington, in the Allen Buick; Stockton Veazey, H.H. Durston & Dr. D.J. Macdonald in the Veazey Ford; Mr. & Mrs. J. P. Stagg & Mr. & Mrs. W.J. Allen in the Stagg Winton; W.M. Montgomery, Frank Toole, J.C. Keppler & William Wraith in the Montgomery Winton; F.T. Ford, H.G. Coy, C.C. Hall, R.B. Abbott & D.O. Noel in the Hall Reo; W.L. Collins, H.A. Conyne, G.W. Sparrow, W.H. Mahoney & Frank Osborn in the Osborn Studebaker; Dr. & Mrs. H.F. Carman & Mr. & Mrs. C.R. Fuller in the Carman Oakland; W.W. Harper, W.A. Bower, E.E. Moore, D. Kaufman & Phillip O'Neil in the Branscombe Ford.

19. Letter to the Deerlodge National Forest from Bankers' Surety Company dated September 24, 1910, Montana State Archives (Montana State Hospital—Warm Springs).

20. Bond between the Allen Company and Bankers Surety Company dated November 8, 1910, Montana State Archives (Montana State Hospital—Warm Springs). Prices listed included $4 per M for timber and telephone poles, 10 cents for converter poles, 3 cents for 16-foot lagging poles, 2.5 cents for 12-foot lagging poles, 50 cents per cord for firewood, and 1 cent for fence posts. A clause in the contract required a modification in the prices based on the average values on January 1, 1913.

21. *Anaconda Standard*, December 18, 1910.

22. Ibid., January 20, 1911.

23. Ibid., February 19, 1911.

24. Letter from John D. Ryan to D.A. Welch dated March 30, 1911, Montana State Archives (Montana State Hospital—Warm Springs).

25. Letter from H.M. Stevenson and W.R. Allen dated April 4, 1911, and an agreement for sale dated April 7, 1911, Montana State Archives (Montana State Hospital—Warm Springs).

26. A letter from the Anaconda Copper Mining Company legal department to W.R. Allen dated April 4, 1911, Montana State Archives (Montana State Hospital—Warm Springs).

27. A letter from A.W. Allen to the District Forester dated April 15, 1911, Record Group 95, National Archives.

28. A letter from Forest Supervisor Mason to the District Forester dated April 15, 1911, Record Group 95, National Archives.

29. A letter from the Acting District Forester to the Forester dated April 15, 1911, Record Group 95, National Archives.

30. Ibid.

31. Montana Historical Society, William R. Allen photograph collection; *Progressive Men of the State of Montana*. A.W. Bowen & Co., 1900., pp. 1628–9; Wirtz, Shirley and Lorene Lovell, 1976, *One Man's Dream – Elkhorn Mine – Coolidge, Montana,* pp. 20–22. This publication presents a discussion of Allen's effort to develop the Elkhorn Mine and railroad. It also provides information on the town of Coolidge, Montana.

32. Howard, A.G., *The Saga of Nels Pearson – Montana's Paul Bunyan*, Granite County Museum; US Inflation calculator: 1635–2022, Department of Labor data: https://www.in2013dollars.com.

33. *Anaconda Standard*, June 7, 1911.

34. Ibid., December 14, 1913.

35. Ibid., August 10, 1913.

36. Map of French Gulch logging operation, 1905–1912.

37. *Anaconda Standard*, December 14, 1913.

38. Surety Bond dated December 30, 1916; letter from the District Forester F.A. Silcox to Deerlodge National Forest Supervisor dated December 30, 1917, Montana French Gulch, record Group 95, National Archives.

Chapter Sixteen
Fire in the Woods

1. *Semi-Weekly Miner*, May 19, 1886.

2. Ibid.

3. Ibid., July 11, 1886; *Weekly Anaconda Review*, July 15, 1886.

4. *Semi-Weekly Inter Mountain*, August 25, 1886.

5. Ibid.; *Semi-Weekly Miner*, August 25, 1886.

6. *Semi-Weekly Inter Mountain*, August 29, 1886.

7. *Semi-Weekly Miner*, September 25, 1886; US Inflation calculator: 1635–2022, Department of Labor data: https://www.in2013dollars.com.

8. *Weekly Anaconda Review*, October 14, 1886; Department of Labor data: https://www.in2013dollars.com

9. Ibid.

10. Personal study of the 1889 fire year.

11. *Semi-Weekly Miner*, August 10, 1889.

12. Ibid., August 21, 1889.

13. Ibid., August 28, 1889; *Helena Daily Independent*, August 24, 1889.

14. *Semi-Weekly Miner*, August 31, 1889.

15. Ibid., September 4; *Anaconda Standard*, September 10, 1889.

16. *Anaconda Standard*, September 15, and September 30, 1889.

17. Ibid., October 8, 1889.

18. Ibid., October 1, 1890.

19. Ibid., July 19, 1899.

20. Ibid., August 2, and August 4, 1900.

21. Ibid., August 1, 13, 15, 17, 1901.

22. Ibid., September 8,9,11, 1902.

23. Ibid., August 24, 1903.

24. Ibid., January 20, 1911.

25. Ibid., August 22, 1910.

26. Ibid., August 27, 1910.

Chapter Seventeen
Living in the Woods

1. Personal observations.

2. Ibid.

3. The store was a major source of income for the McCune operation and Henry felt that was where the company made their money rather than the cordwood. Deposition by Henry Geigerich in case P-45899, File 2002.003.346, pp. 93 & 94, National Museum of Forest Service History.

4. *Anaconda Recorder*, November 10, 1894.

5. A part of McCune's operation that was north of the Continental Divide could not be surveyed as it is primarily private land with limited public access. After consulting old maps of the three logging areas, a field investigation was undertaken to locate cabins or other features. Several cabins shown on these maps were not found and in other cases only a flattened spot or some remaining pieces could be found. Consequently, the figures shown represent what were present at the time of the survey rather than the actual number and an estimate of construction type of the original buildings.

6. Box or hog trough corner is listed as a western innovation. It consisted of constructing a panel of logs held together by a two-by-ten board at each end. The boards of the panels were then joined to form a corner. Jordan, Terry G., Jon T. Kilpinen, Charles F. Gritzner, *The Mountain West: Interpreting the Folk Landscape Cabin Styles,* 1997.

7. One explanation for the lack of cans could be that they were taken to Butte and used to collect dissolved minerals from wastewater. Cans were added to the water and the dissolved mineral would precipitate out on the can and could be recovered. Children in Butte and Anaconda made spending money by collecting cans for the company.

8. Information on population numbers and place of origin were obtained from US census data for the years 1870, 1880, 1900, and 1910.

9. *New Northwest Weekly*, April 13, 1883.

10. *Semi-Weekly Miner*, April 14, 1883; US Inflation calculator: 1635–2022, Department of Labor data: https://www.in2013dollars.com.

11. Crofutt's Anaconda Business Directory for 1885–6, Supplemental; City Directories Butte-Anaconda, Butte-Silver Bow Public Archives, Butte, Montana.

12. *Anaconda Standard*, July 16,1893.

13. Sorden, L.G. & Jacque Vallier, January 1, 1986, *Lumberjack Lingo: A Dictionary of the Logging Era.* The game rooster fight involved a broom handle placed under the knees of a squatting man with his hands tied to it on either side. Two men tied in this fashion butted each other to see who would get tipped over first. Other games are described in this book.

14. Ibid., p. 70.

15. Cabin 172 – On McCune logging area.

16. *Anaconda Standard*, July 31, 1892.

17. Ibid., March 10, 1894.

18. Flanagan, Darris, 2003, *Skid Trails: Glory Days of Montana Logging.* Stoneydale Press Publishing Co., Stevenville, Montana, p. 93.

19. *Semi-Weekly Miner*, December 29, 1883.

20. *Anaconda Standard*, December 29, 1889.

21. Ibid., July 14, 1891.

22. Ibid., May 7, 1891.

23. Ibid., June 4, 1905.

24. *Semi-Weekly Miner*, December 2, 1882

25. Ibid., May 31, 1882.

26. *Anaconda Standard*, July 16, 1893.

27. Ibid., August 3, 1892.

28. Information on woods injuries was obtained from a review of the following papers: *Semi-Weekly Miner*, *Anaconda Standard*, *New Northwest*, and *Helena Daily Independent* between 1882 and 1915. While the number of deaths is probably close to the actual number that occurred during the time period, the number of injuries is probably understated.

29. *Anaconda Standard*, May 30, 1905.

Chapter Eighteen
Settlement of Past Sins

1. Letter from Luther T. Hauberg to the Commissioner, General Land Office, dated August 30, 1909, in case P-45899, pp. 42–44, Record Group 60, Department of Justice, National Archives.

2. Letter from A.W. Lafferty to Commissioner, General Land Office, dated July 6, 1906, in case P-45899, pp. 39 & 40, Record Group 60, Department of Justice, National Archives; US Inflation calculator: 1635–2022, Department of Labor data: https://www.in2013dollars.com.

3. Letter from Louis Sharp to Commissioner, General Land Office, dated January 13, 1908, in case P-45899, pp. 8–10, Record Group 60.

4. Ibid.

5. *Semi-Weekly Miner*, April 30, 1878.

6. Letter from Louis Sharp to Commissioner, General Land Office, dated July 24, 1908, Record Group 60, Department of Justice, National Archives.

7. Letter from Louis Sharp to Commissioner, General Land Office, dated August 22, 1908, pp. 72–73, Record Group 60, Department of Justice, National Archives; US Inflation calculator: 1635–2022, Department of Labor data: https://www.in2013dollars.com.

8. Report by Edward Doyle to Commissioner, General Land Office, dated June 30, 1908, pp. 189–193; Report by L.S. Ropes to Commissioner, General Land Office, dated June 29, 1908, pp. 194–198; Report by Edward Doyle to Commissioner, General Land Office, dated August 23, 1908, pp. 200–206, in case P-45899, Record Group 60, Department of Justice, National Archives.

9. Letter from Edward Doyle to Commissioner, General Land Office, dated August 23, 1908, in case P-45899 pp. 75–79, Record Group 60, Department of Justice, National Archives.

10. Table of Results of the McCune Trespass survey, in case P-45899, pp. 171–175, Record Group 60, Department of Justice, National Archives.

11. Report from Louis Sharp to Commissioner, General Land Office dated January 15, 1909, pp. 99–114, Record Group 60, Department of Justice, National Archives.

12. Letter from Louis Sharp to Commissioner, General Land Office dated January 18, 1909, in case P-45899, p. 94, Record Group 60, Department of Justice, National Archives.

13. Hall, Frank, *Memorandum for the Department in Re offer of Compromise in case of United States V. James B. Haggin,* August 29, 1913, case 150403, Record Group 60, Department of Justice, National Archives.

14. Letter from Howard J. Atwell to Commissioner, General Land Office dated June 30, 1909, in case P-45899, pp. 27–36, Record Group 60, Department of Justice, National Archives.

15. Ibid.

16. Hall, Frank, *Memorandum for the Department in Re offer of Compromise in Case of United States V. James B. Haggin,* August 29, 1913, case 150403, Record Group 60, Department of Justice, National Archives.

17. Ibid.

18. Ibid.

19. Letter from special Agent Luther T. Hauberg to Commissioner, General Land Office, dated August 1909 in case P-45899, pp. 92–93, Record Group 60, Department of Justice, National Archives.

20. Record of timber sales on the Deerlodge National Forest from 1906, Deerlodge National Forest. On August 21, 1907, Nels Pearson obtained a timber sale for 24,205,000 bf. in the Willow Creek Drainage.

21. Letter from Louis Sharp to Commissioner, General Land Office, dated September 4, 1909, in case P-45899, p. 210, Record Group 60, Department of Justice, National Archives.

22. Letter from Louis Sharp to Commissioner, General Land Office, dated December 15, 1909, in case P-45899, pp. 1–7, Record Group 60, Department of Justice, National Archives.

23. Ibid.

24. US Inflation calculator: 1635–2022, Department of Labor data: https://www.in2013dollars.com.

25. Letter from Frank Hall to Assistant Attorney General Ernest Knaebel dated July 23, 1912, marked 150403, Record Group 60, Department of Justice, National Archives.

26. Letter from Frank Hall to Attorney General dated November 19, 1912, marked 150403-46, Record Group 60, Department of Justice, National Archives.

27. Ibid.

28. Ibid.

29. Letter from Frank Hall to Attorney General dated July 23, 1913, marked 150403-72, Record Group 60, Department of Justice, National Archives.

30. Hill, James Madison, *Report on lands in Townships 3 and 4 North, Ranges 11 and 12 West, Deerlodge National Forest, Montana,* 1913. Record Group 60, Department of Justice case file 150403, National Archives.

31. Hall, Frank, *Memorandum for the Department in Re offer of Compromise in Case of United States V. James B. Haggin,* August 29, 1913, case 150403 and a letter from Frank Hall to the Attorney General dated July 23, 1913, case 150403-72, Record Group 60, Department of Justice, National Archives.

32. Ibid.; US Inflation calculator: 1635–2022, Department of Labor data: https://www.in2013dollars.com.

33. Letter from the firm of Alexander & Green to Frank Hall dated July 22, 1913, case 150403, Record Group 60, Department of Justice, National Archives.

34. Letter from Frank Hall to Attorney General dated February 25, 1914, case 150403-103, Record Group 60, Department of Justice, National Archives.

35. Letter from F.A. Reeves to Attorney General dated April 17, 1914, case 150403-115, Record Group 60, Department of Justice, National Archives.

36. Memorandum for Mr. Wallace from unknown dated March 26, 1914, case 150403, Record Group 60, Department of Justice, National Archives.

37. Letter from F.A. Reeves to Attorney General dated April 17, 1914, and May 1, 1914, case 150403-115, Record Group 60, Department of Justice, National Archives.

38. Letter from Ernest Knaebel, Assistant Attorney General to Britton & Gray Attorneys and Counselors of Law dated May 6, 1914, case 150403-110, Record Group 60, Department of Justice, National Archives.

39. Letter from Frank Hall to Attorney General dated January 4, 1915, case 150403-123, Record Group 60, Department of Justice, National Archives.

Chapter Nineteen
Epilogue

1. MacMillan, Donald, *Smoke Wars: Anaconda Copper, Montana air pollution, and the courts, 1890-1920,* 2000, pp. 150–152.

2. Ibid., p. 168.

3. Ibid., p. 203.

4. Ibid., p. 213.

5. Ibid., pp. 252–253.

6. Ibid., pp. 255–256.

7. Personal observation.

8. Historical Research Associates, *Historic resources study Mount Haggin area Deer Lodge County, Montana,* June 30, 1980, Missoula, Montana, p. 94.

9. Personal observation.

References

Books, Articles & Reports

Allen, William R. 1949. *The Chequemegon.* The William-Frederick Press, New York.

Angel, Myron, ed. 1881. *History of Nevada: With Illustrations and Biographical Sketches of Its Prominent Men and Pioneers.* Thompson & West, Oakland, CA.

Berthold, Mary Paddock. 1973. *Big Hole Journal: Notes and Excerpts.* Harlo Press, Detroit, MI.

Bruce, Eugene S. *Flumes and Fluming.* June 4, 1914. Bulletin of the US Department of Agriculture No. 87. Government Printing Office, Washington, DC.

Butcher, Edward Bernie. 1965. *An Analysis of Timber Depredations in Montana to 1900.* M.A. thesis, Eastern Montana College.

Deer Lodge County History Group. 1975. *In (Under) the Shadow of Mount Haggin: The Story of Anaconda and Deer Lodge County from 1863 to 1976.* Anaconda, MT.

Drummond, James. 1997. *The History of Mount Haggin Livestock Company and the Drummond Family on the Ranch.* Manuscript, Bozeman, MT.

Flanagan, Darris. 2003. *Skid Trails: Glory Days of Montana Logging.* Stoneydale Press Publishing Co., Stevensville, MT.

Gilluly, Jack. December 1991. *Haggin's Cross-Country Snowbirds Serve Up Local Historical Fare.* Draft of an article in *Montana Magazine*, Helena, MT.

Glasscock, C.B. 1966, 1935. *The War of the Copper Kings.* Grosset & Dunlap, New York.

Gordon, Greg. 2014. *When Money Grew on Trees.* University of Oklahoma Press, Norman, OK.

Howard, A.G. n.d. *The Saga of Nels Pearson – Montana's Paul Bunyan.* Philipsburg Historical Society, Philipsburg, MT, p. 6.

Johnson, Florence Riddle. 1964. *Ghost Trails Country.* Published by author, Anaconda, MT.

Jordan, Terry G., Jon T. Kilpinen, Charles F. Gritzner, 1997. *The Mountain West: Interpreting the Folk Landscape Cabin Styles.* The John Hopkins University Press, Baltimore, MD.

Kelly, Matt J. 1983. *Anaconda, Montana's Copper City.* Soroptimist Club of Anaconda, Anaconda, MT.

Kramer, E.W. August 21, 1912. *Report to District Forester on data obtained on the Allen Flume near Anaconda, Montana, and on the Rochet Flume near St. Joe, Idaho,* DE – Reports, Logging Flumes, Missoula, MT.

Kroninger, Robert, *The Justice and the Lady*, In the Yearbook 1977, Supreme Court Historical Society, Washington, DC.

MacMillan, Donald. 2000. *Smoke Wars: Anaconda Copper, Montana Air Pollution, and the Courts 1890–1920.* Creasey Printing, Springfield, IL.

Malone, Michael P. 1981. *The Battle for Butte.* Montana Historical Society Press, Helena, MT.

Marcosson, Isaac F. 1957. *Anaconda*. Dodd, Mead & Co., New York.

Marsh, George D. *Copper Camp*. 1970, 1943. Riverbend Publishing, Helena, MT, p. 325.

Mason, D. T. July 12, 1915. *Utilization and Management of Lodgepole Pine in the Rocky Mountains*. Bulletin of the US Department of Agriculture No. 234. Government Printing Office, Washington, DC.

McNelis, Sarah. 2018. *The Biography of F. Augustus Heinze: Copper King at War*. University of Montana Press, Missoula, MT.

Miller, Joaquin. 1894. *An Illustrated History of the State of Montana*. Lewis Publishing Co., Chicago, IL.

Mogenson, Paul. 2015. *Timber Trespass Lawsuits*. Draft Paper. p. 14. Hamilton, MT.

Mutschler, Charles V. 2002. *Wired for Success: The Butte, Anaconda & Pacific Railway, 1892–1985*. Washington State University Press, Pullman, WA.

Pierce, C.J., R.E. Swain, & J.P. Mitchell. February 5, 1913. *Report on the Effects of Smelter Smoke on Vegetation and the Condition of the National Forests in the Vicinity of Anaconda, MT.* Presented to the Department of Justice.

Pinchot, Gifford. 1947. *Breaking New Ground*. Island Press, Washington, DC.

Ramsdell, H.J. October 25, 2009. *The Great Nevada Flume*. From Henry T. Williams, *The Pacific Tourist, Adams & Bishop's Illustrated Trans-Continental Guide* (1881) pp. 219–224. In: *The Nevada Observer* December 25, 2009.

Taylor, Bill & Jan. 1998. *The Butte Short Line*. Pictorial Histories Publishing Co., Missoula, MT.

Taylor, Bill & Jan. 1999. *Rails to Gold and Silver*. Pictorial Histories Publishing Co., Missoula, MT.

Thomas Bill & Marilyn. 1997. *Elliston: Days Gone By*. Century Lithography, Helena, MT.

Thompson & West's *History of Nevada 1881, with Illustrations and Biographical Sketches of its Prominent Men and Pioneers,* Chapter XXIV "Transportation of Lumber by Water." In: *The Nevada Observer,* December 8, 2005.

Toole, Kenneth Ross. "The Anaconda Copper Mining Company, A Price war and a copper corner." *Pacific Northwest Quarterly*. October 1950, pp. 313–329.

USDI General Land Office. 1909. Correspondence, 92-45899 in A.W. McCune Timber Trespass, Hellgate Forest Reserve. Case 150403, Justice File 144276, Record Group 60, Box 365-987. The National Archives, Washington, DC.

Vogel, Frank. 1910. *A.C.M. Timber Survey, Upper Deer Lodge Valley*. Anaconda/Deer Lodge Historical Society Archives, Anaconda, MT.

Walsh, Natalie, and Gael Bissell. February 1979. *Impact of Copper Smelter Emissions on Two Subalpine Ecosystems Near Anaconda, Montana*. Report No. 79-7, Forest Insect & Disease Management, USDA, Forest Service, Northern Region, Missoula, MT.

Wells, Arthur E. n.d. *Report of the Anaconda Smoke Commission Covering the Period from May 1, 1911 to October 1, 1920.* Justice File 144276. The National Archives, Washington DC.

Wegars, Priscilla. 1991. *Who's Been Workin' on the Railroad?: An Examination of the Construction, Distribution, and Ethnic Origins of Domed Rock Ovens on Railroad-Related Sites.* Historical Archaeology, Vol. 25, No. 1, pp. 37–65

Whitney, Orson Ferguson. 1892. *History of Utah*. Vol. IV, Biographical. George Q. Cannon & Sons Co., Salt Lake, UT.

Williams, Gerald W. July 2000. *The USDA Forest Service – The First Century*. FS-650, USDA Forest Service, Washington, DC.

Wirtz, Shirley and Lorene Lovell. 1976. *One Man's Dream: Elkhorn Mine, Coolidge, Montana.* Aston Printing Co., Butte, MT.

Progressive Men of the State of Montana. 1900. A.W. Bowen & Co., Chicago, IL.

Historic Resources Study Mount Haggin Area Deer Lodge County, Montana. 1980. Prepared for Montana Department of Fish, Wildlife, and Parks by Historical Research Associates, Missoula, MT.

Angel, Myron, ed. 1881. *History of Nevada with Illustrations and Biographical Sketches of its Prominent Men and Pioneers.* Thompson & West, Oakland, CA.

Ceofutt's Anaconda Business Directory for 1885-6. Supplemental; City Directories Butte-Anaconda.

Forbes, Reginald D., ed. 1956. *Forestry Handbook.* The Ronald Press Co., New York.

Thompson, Jessie, ed. *Early Days in the Forest Service*, Vol. 1. ca. 1944. USDA, Forest Service, Northern Region, Missoula, MT.

Transportation of Lumber by Water: From Chapter 24, Thompson & West's History of Nevada 1881. Reprinted in *The Nevada Observer,* December 8, 2005.

Writers' Program. 1970, 1943. *Copper Camp,* Riverbend Publishing, Helena, MT.

Newspapers

Anaconda Recorder
Anaconda Standard
Arizona Daily Star
Butte Daily Post
Butte Miner
Daily Inter-Mountain
Daily Yellowstone Journal
Helena Daily Independent
Iowaville Roster
Missoula Gazette
Missoulian
New Northwest
Oakland Tribune
Semi-Weekly Inter Mountain
Semi-Weekly Miner
The Billings Gazette
The Nevada Observer
Weekly Anaconda Review

Census

US Department of the Interior. Census Office. *Ninth Census of the United States 1870.*

US Department of the Interior. Census Office. *Tenth Census of the United States 1880.*

US Department of the Interior. Census Office. *Twelfth Census of the United States 1900.*

US Department of the Interior. Census Office. *Thirteenth Census of the United States 1910.*

Web Sites

US Inflation calculator: 1635-2022, Department of Labor Data: https://www.in2013dollars.com

Information on horse capabilities, https://www.horseforum.com.

Wikipedia contributors. "David Neagle," Wikipedia, The Free Encyclopedia, https://en.wikipedia.org/w/index.php?title=David_Neagle&oldid=953072733 (accessed May 28, 2020).

Manuscript Collections

———, Anaconda-Deer Lodge Historical Society, Anaconda, MT.

———, Butte-Silver Bow Public Archives, Butte, MT.

———, Montana Historical Society, MC169, Box No. 1, 52, 124, 134, 409, 415, 416, & 276; and MC105, William Allen papers, Helena, MT.

———, Montana State Archives (Montana State Hospital—Warm Springs). Helena, MT.

———, National Archives, Record Group 60, Records of the Department of Justice, Case P-45899.

———, National Archives, Record Group 95, Sales, Deerlodge National Forest.

———, National Museum of Forest Service History, File 2002.003.346; File 2002.003.353-354. Missoula, MT.

———, Record of timber sales on the Deerlodge National Forest from 1906 to 1923, USDA Forest Service, Deerlodge National Forest. Butte, MT.

Maps

Patten, J.M., Map of the Allen Co. Timber Sale of 9/12/06, Deerlodge Nat'al Forest. Mount Haggin Wildlife Management Area.

———, Map of French Gulch logging operation 1905-1912. Mount Haggin Wildlife Management Area.

———, Map of Butte, Anaconda & Pacific Railroad, Butte-Silver Bow Public Archives, Butte, MT.

———, Map of mining claims owned by Allen in the French Gulch area. 1903. From Allen Gold Mining Company pp. 8-9.

Appendix A – Flumes

Flume Name	**Flume Length**	**Flume Grade**	**Flume Size**
McCune Operation			
Original Main McCune	10.3 miles	2.8 percent	34"x42"
Main Flume Extended	23 miles*	2 percent	34"x42"
West Mill Creek	4.1 miles**	3.1 percent**	Unknown
Clear Creek	3 miles**	8.3 percent**	Unknown
Sevenmile Creek	1.5 miles	6 percent	18"x25"
Tenmile Creek	1.27 miles	3 percent	18"x25"
Lower Tenmille Creek	0.67 miles	7.5 percent	18"x25"
Allen Operation			
Main Allen	10 miles	1.5 percent	34"x42"
Reused McCune section	5.95 miles	4.2 percent	34"x42"
Little California Creek	1.5 miles	11.4 percent	12"x?"
American Creek	1.8 miles	2 percent	12"x?"
Little American Creek	0.48 miles**	5.3 percent**	Unknown
Willow Creek Operation			
Main Willow Creek	5.5 miles**	3.7 percent	34"x42"**
Long Canyon	1.51 miles	9.2 percent	unknown
West Fork, North branch	2.21 miles	8.7 percent	unknown
West Fork, South branch	.85 miles	8.8 percent	unknown
West Fork, Unnamed branch (probable)	.52 miles**	13.6 percent	unknown

* Distance excludes 3.5 miles of the original flume and runs from Mill Creek Station to Twelvemile Creek.

** Estimated values

Appendix B – Trams & Chutes

Tram Name	Type	Length	Grade	Elev. gain	Location
McCune Operation					
East Sugarloaf	Horse	3516 ft	4%		SE ¼ Sec 15 T3N R11W
West Willow	Horse	3667 ft	3.3%		NE ¼ Sec 15 T3N R11W
Sauna House	Horse	5280 ft	2.5%		NE ¼ Sec 16 T3N R11W
Lower Sawmill	Unknown	1700 ft**			SW ¼ Sec 10 T3N R11W
Upper Sawmill	Unknown	3400 ft**			NE ¼ Sec 16 T3N R11W
West Willow	Hoist	1649 ft		122ft	NW ¼ Sec 15 T3N R11W
Sawmill-Camp	Descent	1642 ft		280ft	NW ¼ Sec 15 T3N R11W
California Creek	Hoist	2900 ft		226ft	NE ¼ Sec 17 T3N R11W
California Horse	Horse	7920 ft**	2%		SE ¼ Sec 16 T3N R11W
Oregon Creek	Hoist	2640 ft		230ft	SW ¼ Sec 17 T3N R11W
Oregon Creek Horse	Horse	500 ft **			SW ¼ Sec 17 T3N R11W
East Two Tram	Hoist	2520 ft		300ft	SE ¼ Sec 18 T3N R11W
West Two Tram	Hoist	2520 ft		310ft	SE ¼ Sec 18 T3N R11W
Upper Tenmile Creek	Hoist	4470 ft		391ft	E ½ Sec 10 T3N R12W
Lower Tenmile Creek	Hoist	4674 ft		468ft	W ½ Sec 14 T3N R12W
Corral Creek	Hoist	3640 ft		425ft	SW ¼ Sec 9 T3N R12W
Corral Creek Horse	Horse	2640 ft	3%		NW ¼ Sec 16 T3N R12W
Slaughter Creek	Horse	3500+ ft**	0%		NE ¼ Sec 16 T3N R12W
Log Chute	Decent	2340 ft**		739 ft	SW ¼ Sec 29 T4N R 11W

Allen Operation					
Bridge-Sawmill	Hoist	2475 ft		320ft	SW ¼ Sec 22 T3N R11W
Bridge-Crooked John	Hoist	4285 ft		40ft	SE ¼ Sec 21 T3N R11W
Crooked-California	Horse	6600 ft**	1.5%		Sec 21 T3N R11W
Crooked John	Hoist	4980 ft		475ft	NE ¼ Sec 28 T3N R11W
Little American	Hoist	6600 ft		570ft	NW ¼ Sec 33 T3N R11W
Log Chute	Descent	1870 ft**		520ft	NE ¼ Sec 4 T2N R11W

Willow Creek Operation
No trams were used in this operation, as all of the flumes were adjacent to a stream.

** Estimated values

Appendix C – List of employees of Caplice & McCune camped in the mountains 1885-1886

A

Acord, Con, teamster
Adams, John, blacksmith
Ainslee, G., laborer
Allen E., H., teamster
Anderson, F.T., wood chopper
Anderson, John, laborer
Anderson P., wood chopper
Anderson S., laborer
Anstengstall, William, laborer

B

Baldwin, W.J., wood chopper
Baker, J.R., wood chopper
Barric, A., teamster
Berger, Frank, wood chopper
Bickford, G.B., cook
Birte, Antone, laborer
Black, Hugh, wood chopper
Bledsoe, George, wood chopper
Boyd, C.J., laborer
Browning, B., teamster
Byers, James, laborer
Bywns, J., teamster

C

Calaran, J.W., wood chopper

Campbell, J., teamster

Canlson, T., laborer

Capp, A.B., wood chopper

Carlson, Jno., wood chopper

Carpenter, C.C., wood chopper

Claridge, S.D., teamster

Closteman, C. H., wood chopper

Collins, V., teamster

Comstock, O., wood chopper

Conway, J., teamster

Concrite, G.W., teamster

Cook, Charles, cook

Cook, C., teamster

Crafton, C.O., teamster

Cronan, Con, teamster

D

Daily, J., teamster

Dargarel, Thos., laborer

Dawson, George, wood chopper

Daxon, R., teamster

Daxon, W., teamster

Deardorff, S.R., wood chopper

Delaney, W., wood chopper

Dickenson, George, teamster

Dodge, E.O., wood chopper

Doyle, W., wood chopper

Dudley, C. H., laborer

Dunlane, ——, wood chopper

Dunlap, A.C., wood chopper

E

Evans, Jno., wood chopper

F

Faust, C., teamster

Faust, J., teamster

Fay, Frank, teamster

Furgeson, J.C., wood chopper

G

Gallagher, ——, wood chopper

Gastwold, Jno., laborer

Gerty, Owen, laborer

Gibbons, P., teamster

Gilmore, P., teamster

Gleason, Jno., wood chopper

Gleason, J., teamster

Goana, J., teamster

Grant, M.A., blacksmith

Gray, W.H., wood chopper

Grobb, Jacob, wood chopper

Gergrich, M.S., clerk

H

Hackkal, Jacob, wood chopper

Hall, T., teamster

Hanlon, Jas., wood chopper

Hansan, H., teamster

Harigan, P., teamster

Hart, H., teamster

Hartle, R., teamster

Hartle, R., teamster

Hartley, James, cook

Hankins, J., wagon maker

Hauld, Jos., wood chopper

Hauld, M.H., wood chopper

Heiser, G.L., wood chopper

Hennessy, J.C., wood chopper

Hoffman, Peter, wood chopper

Hogan, Thos., laborer

Hoyness, D., teamster

Hoyt, E.B., laborer

Huff, F.M., wood chopper

Hull, S., teamster

Hunt, George, wood chopper

J

Jackson, J., laborer

Jacobs, J., teamster

Jakins, H., wood chopper

James, Robert, laborer

Jantika, H., wood chopper

Jim ——, helper to the cook

Johnson, C., wood chopper

Johnson, E., teamster

Johnson, P.L., wood chopper

Johnson, S., teamster

Jones, J., teamster

K

Kari, Gus, wood chopper

Karppi, Chs., laborer

Kelly, E.L., wood chopper

Kelley, George, wood chopper

Kelley, Jas., Wood chopper

Kelley, J., teamster

King, Jno., wood chopper

Kinney, J., wood chopper

L

Landers, M., teamster

Laycock, M., wood chopper

LeMier, Jas., wood chopper

Lewis, T., teamster

Lockhart, C.M., laborer

Long, Pat, teamster

Lundberg, C., laborer

Lynn, Chs., wood chopper

M

Mack, James, wood chopper

Mangum, J.H., clerk

Martina, J., teamster

McCall, T., laborer

McCall, T., teamster

McClosky, B., laborer
McCready, W., teamster
McCune, E.I., clerk
McCune, M., harnessmaker
McDonough, C.S., wood chopper
McGilvery, Jno., laborer
McGinnis, D., teamster
McGunn, J., teamster
McKenney, G., teamster
McMillan, C., teamster
Melas, Mike, wood chopper
Mieir, A., teamster
Miller, J., teamster
Mink, F.S., teamster
Mitchel, Frank, laborer
Mitchel, Peter, laborer
Moore, Wm., laborer
Morgan, Wm., teamster
Morise, German, wood chopper
Mosby, O., laborer
Moseby, D., laborer

N

Neff, J., teamster
Nelson, N.H., teamster

O

Ogden, W., laborer
Ogden, W., teamster
Oiste, Jno., laborer
Olesen, Ed, wood chopper
Orme, A., teamster

P

Passenger, Mike, laborer
Pehleyamac, Matt, wood chopper
Pell, Chs., laborer
Perry, D., teamster
Picards, J., laborer

Pickovich, L., wood chopper
Piper, W.G., freighter
Potter, G.D., wagon maker
Pratt, David, teamster
Primach, Nick, wood chopper
Pullman, A., teamster

Q

Queen, W.A., wood chopper

R

Ramlet, A., teamster
Rammell, C., teamster
Rapp, George, teamster
Rasmusser, T., laborer
Raux, Frank, wood chopper
Redmond, P., teamster
Revie, Chs., wood chopper
Reynolds, Thos., laborer
Rider, Jno., laborer
Ritter, Jno., D. bookkeeper
Roach, C., teamster
Robinson, H., wood chopper
Rogers, H.L., wood chopper
Rollins, M., teamster
Rollins, R., teamster
Rook, R., teamster
Rowan, G., teamster
Rummels, J., teamster
Ryan, B., laborer
Ryan, Dan, teamster

S

Sanders, Dan, laborer
Sanders, H., laborer
Sanders, H., laborer
Scullon, Pat, wood chopper
Shanghnessey, T., laborer
Sheldon, Smith, laborer

Shepherd, Wm., laborer
Sherridan, C.C., teamster
Shields, P, laborer
Simasard, Therance, woodchopper
Sloan, W.K., merchant
Small, M., laborer
Small, W.W., carpenter
Smith, B.O., wood chopper
Smith, Chas., laborer
Smith, Lewis, laborer
Soughtford, Wm., wood chopper
Sparks, E.H., freighter
Sherlock, J.C., surveyor
St. Amant, Eugene, wood chopper
Sutherland, H., teamster
Sutterfield, C.S., wood chopper

T

Taylor, C., teamster
Thorp, W., teamster
Tibbitts, J., teamster
Tibbetts, Jno., laborer
Tobin, P., teamster
Tucker, ——, wood chopper

V

Vermost, J., clerk
Vickory, Thos., laborer

W

Wagner, D., wood chopper
Walker, Thos. D., wood chopper
Wallace, A., teamster
Wallace, J., teamster
Ward, A., wood chopper
Webster, H., laborer
Welch, W.R., teamster
Wendell, J., laborer
Whalen, J., laborer

Wild, J., teamster
Wild, M., teamster
Wilson, Dick, teamster
Wysong, W.H., wood chopper

Y

Yarborough, T.J., teamster
Yimalt, J., teamster

OCCUPATION

Teamster	83
Wood chopper	72
Laborer	51
Clerk	4
Cook	3
Cook helper	1
Blacksmith	2
Wagon maker	2
Freighter	2
Harnessmaker	1
Bookkeeper	1
Merchant	1
Carpenter	1
Surveyor	1

Total crew = 225

Appendix D – List of Employees in Allen's Camp 2—1910

A

Adams, Raffachel, Italy, wood chopper

Anderson, Issac, Finland, wood chopper

Anolile, Samial, Italy, wood chopper

Anselmo, Bernadi, Italy, wood chopper

Atilio, Bulazi, Italy, wood chopper

B

Baech, Peter, Austria, wood chopper

Bales, Mike, Austria, fluming

Bartolomei, ——, Italy, wood chopper

Beske, George, Austria, laborer

Bohnn, John, Austria, carpenter

Broohes, B. Joseph, US, wood chopper

Burlier, John, Austria, laborer

C

Chareson, Elmer, Sweden, wood chopper

Cullen, Michel, US, teamster

D

Dalfriz, Thomas, Austria, wood chopper

Doene, Christin, Italy, laborer

Domenico, Peter, Italy, wood chopper

Dorgmach, Valetine, Italy, wood chopper

Doris, Nicklos, Austria, wood chopper

Douglass, G. Joseph, US, wood chopper
Dudley, Harold, US, wood chopper

E

Englerth, John J., US, Forest Ranger
Eskrich, Michiel, Austria, wood chopper

F

Ferrette, Frank, Italy, wood chopper
Fontana, Raffechil, Italy, wood chopper
Fontana, Sabustino, Italy, wood chopper
Foran, John, Canada, carpenter
Fredrana, Agustino, Italy, wood chopper

G

Genderson, John, Norway, laborer
Gertruse, Guseppe, Italy, wood chopper
Gioronale, Basilo, Italy, wood chopper
Gorman, Andrew, US, teamster
Grabatck, Stanely, Russia, fluming
Gulfe, Louis, Austria, laborer

H

Harrison, C.W., Canada, wood chopper
Hayes, Nathen, US, foreman
Heater, O.L., US, superintendent of timber camp
Herbert, Jake, Poland, fluming
Hughes, Alfried, US, Forest Ranger

J

James, Emil, Finland, laborer
Johnson, George, Finland, wood chopper
Johnsen, Nicklos, Finland, wood chopper
Jones, Joseph, Italy, wood chopper

K

Kelley, H. Patrick, US, stable foreman
Kolar, Paul, Austria, fluming
Kraus, Andrew, Austria, fluming

L

Larson, Eric, Sweden, wood chopper
Lindsay, T.W., Canada, wood chopper
Lundin, Emil, Sweden, teamster

M

McFadden, ——, US, Forest Ranger
McJonas, R.P., Canada, stationary engineer
Montie, George, Italy, wood chopper
Moreni, Anbrogno, Italy, wood chopper
Moreni, Casimiso, Italy, wood chopper
Moreni, Francisco, Italy, wood chopper
Moreni, Guseffi, Italy, wood chopper
Moreni, Isidore, Italy, wood chopper
Moreni, Ottorsio, Italy, wood chopper
Mossinnio, Ginota, Austria, wood chopper

N

Nettii, Eli, Russia, wood chopper

O

Olire, Ernest, England, teamster
Osam, Edward, Russia, wood chopper
Osam, Mathew, Russia, wood chopper

P

Pardine, Carlo, Italy, wood chopper
Pelegrino, Bacini, Italy, wood chopper
Pelegrino, Rafaelli, Italy, wood chopper
Pelode, Birojenesi, Italy, wood chopper
Pigala, Samial, Austria, wood chopper
Pucete, Adalfo, Italy, wood chopper

R

Ray, Andrew, US, foreman
Ries, Julio D., Wales, salesman general store
Ririlo, Marinio, Italy, wood chopper
Rogoske, Mike, Russia, fluming
Rousseau, Joseph, Canada, wood chopper

S

Sardula, Charles, Austria, fluming
Sarros, Anibale, Austria, wood chopper
Seoba, Alvers, Italy, wood chopper
Sillare, Steren, Italy, wood chopper
Smith, W.E., US, boarding house cook
Smith, Sophie, US, boarding house assistant cook
Smurr, Glen, US, Forest Guard
Soniek, John, Austria, fluming
Sutton, R. William, US, wood chopper
Swikireliore, Somis, Switzerland, boarding house cook

T

Thomas, John, Austria, wood chopper
Timonelli, Francesco, Italy, wood chopper
Tooke, Roscoe C., US, Forest Guard
Trocvutino, Zucconi, Italy, wood chopper
Turkey, Ira, Canada, wood chopper

W

Wina, Henry, Finland, wood chopper

Z

Zawen, Antonio, Austria, wood chopper
Zodak, Mike, Austria, fluming

PLACE OF ORIGIN

US	17
Italy	32
Austria	19
Canada	6
Russia	5
Finland	5
Sweden	3
Norway	1
Poland	1
England	1
Wales	1
Switzerland	1

OCCUPATION	
Wood chopper	57
Fluming	9
Laborer	6
Forest ranger	3
Forest guard	2
Teamster	4
Carpenter	2
Foreman	2
Cook	2
Cook helper	1
Merchant	1
Stable foreman	1
Camp Superintendent	1
Total	92

Appendix E – Forest Service Employees in the Butte Area in 1910

Baird, John, 37, married, from Ireland (1887) – Forester
Cobbs, J.L., 23, single, from Alabama – Forester
Edwards, Charles, 24, single, from Michigan – Forester
Englerth, John, 34, married, from Minnesota – Forest Ranger
Ferguson, R. Trevor, 25, single, from Pennsylvania – Forester
Foster, William J., 29, single, from Montana – Draughtsman (Draftsman) USFS
Green, Charles, 36, married, from Iowa – Forester
Hall, Charles, 39, married, from Illinois – Forest Supervisor Deerlodge Forest
Hughes, Alfried, 31, married, from Missouri – Forest Ranger
Hungate, Harry, 22, married, from Montana – Ranger
McFadden, Mr., 37, single, from Kentucky – Forest Ranger
McKnight, Robert, 34, single, from Michigan – Forest Ranger, Inspector
McLeon Patton, 27, single, from North Carolina – Forester
Miller, James, 32, single, from New Mexico – Ranger
Nelson, Charles, 23, single, from Pennsylvania – Ranger
Pricharrd, Reuben, 25, single, from Massachusetts – Forester
Ranney, George, 38, married, from Montana – Forest Ranger
Saunder, A.C., 23, single, from Massachusetts – Surveyor
Saunders, Aretas, 25, single, from Connecticut – Forester
Schick, Harry, 24, single, from Iowa – Assistant Forest Supervisor Deerlodge Forest
Smith, Foster, 35, married, from Pennsylvania – Ranger
Smurr Glen, 21, single, from Iowa – Forest Guard
Steele, James, 35, married, from Kentucky – Ranger
Stockdale, Lewis, 22, single, from Pennsylvania – Surveyor USFS
Terry, Ellwood, 31, single, from New York – Forester
Tomkins, Frank, 27, single, from New York – Forester
Tooke, Roscoe, 23, single, from Illinois – Forest Guard
John Wherman, 33, married, from Canada – Forest Ranger